Introduction

This book is designed for Year 7 students working at Levels 2 to 4 of the National Curriculum, and is accompanied by a substantial Teacher's Resource. Subsequent books cover Years 8 and 9. These three *Gold* books are an integral part of the *Formula One Maths* series and may be used alongside books A1, B1 and C1 during the three years of Key Stage 3.

The series builds on the National Numeracy Strategy in primary schools and its extension into Key Stage 3. It is designed to support that style of teaching and the lesson framework.

This book is presented as a series of double-page spreads, each of which is designed to be a lesson. The left-hand page covers the material to be taught and the right-hand page provides questions and activities for the students to work through. Each chapter ends with a 'Finishing off' review exercise covering all its content. Further worksheets and ICT materials are provided in the Teacher's Resource.

In addition there are three 'reward' lessons. These contain games (with a mathematical basis) and are for use when students have completed a period of hard work.

A key feature of the left-hand pages is the tasks. These are the main teaching activity for the lesson, and provide opportunities for students to work singly, in pairs, groups, or as a class. The tasks use the students' own experiences to reinforce the teaching for that particular lesson; many of them are based around everyday life. Each of the tasks is supported by a photocopiable task sheet in the Teacher's Resource; these are designed to ensure the time is spent on maths, not on copying out tables and graphs, and to enable students to build up a body of work that they can be proud of.

The left-hand pages include many discussion points. These are designed to help teachers engage their students in whole class discussion. Teachers should see the ? icon as an opportunity and an invitation.

The last part of each lesson is the plenary. The teacher and students discuss what they have been doing and the mathematics involved. This is usually supported by discussion points in the Student's Book, and by quite extensive advice in the Teacher's Resource. The Teacher's Resource also includes lesson objectives, and the plenary is the time to check that these have been met.

The various icons and instructions used in this book are explained overleaf.

The order of the chapters ensures that the subject is developed logically, at each stage building on previous knowledge. The Teacher's Resource includes a scheme of work based on this order. However, teachers are of course free to vary the order to meet their own circumstances and needs.

This series stems from a partnership between Hodder and Stoughton Educational and Mathematics in Education and Industry (MEI).

The authors would like to thank all those who helped in preparing this book, particularly those involved with writing materials for the accompanying Teacher's Resource.

Roger Porkess   2003
Series Editor

How to use this book

 You will have a discussion about this point with your teacher and the rest of the class.

 Use your calculator for this question.

 You are not allowed to use your calculator for this question.

 Your teacher may give you a sheet to write on. This will save time copying out tables and graphs.

⚠ Warning. This is a common mistake. Or, take extra care over this question.

 There is some ICT material in the Teacher's Resource for this work.

This book is a series of double-page spreads. The left-hand page is the teaching page. The right-hand page gives exercise questions, activities or investigations on the topic.

You will also come across the following features.

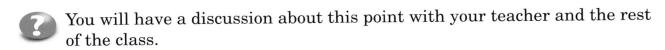

Task

This is the main activity of the lesson. You are expected to spend quite a lot of time on it. It will help you understand the work. Ask your teacher if you need help.

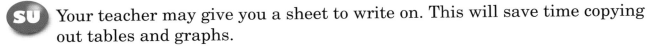

66 Do the right thing!

You are learning something practical. Here are step-by-step instructions to follow.

Contents

1 How our numbers work

Place value

House prices shoot up again

1940	£250
1960	£2 500
1980	£25 000
2000	£250 000

For Sale
£250 000

? **What has happened to the price of this house between 1960 and 1980?**

Notice how the digits move one place to the left when you multiply by 10.

Pete

	M	H Th	T Th	Th	H	T	U	
1940					2	5	0	×10
1960				2	5	0	0	×10
1980			2	5	0	0	0	×10
2000		2	5	0	0	0	0	×10
?	2	5	0	0	0	0	0	×10

? **What is the 2 in the M column worth?**

Task

1 Multiply each number in chart **A** by 10.
Enter the new number in a copy of chart **B**.

A

M	H Th	T Th	Th	H	T	U
			4	0	0	0
			7	2	0	0
		5	1	0	0	0
		9	0	1	6	5
	6	0	0	0	0	0

B

M	H Th	T Th	Th	H	T	U

2 Copy and complete this pattern.
Fill in the missing numbers and words.

Describe the pattern.

6 000 000 =
600 000 = six hundred thousand
60 000 =
 = six thousand
 =
 = sixty
6 = six

? **What happens to the digits when a number is multiplied by 100?**

Exercise

1 **(a)** Copy and complete the place value grid.

1	2	3	4	5	6	7	8	9
10	20	30	40	50				90
100	200		400		600			900
1000		3000		5000			8000	
10 000	20 000					70 000		
100 000	200 000		400 000					

(b) Choose one column.
Explain the number pattern in this column.

2 Copy and complete these sequences.

(a)

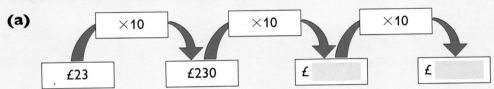

£23 → ×10 → £230 → ×10 → £ → ×10 → £

Describe what happens when numbers are multiplied by 10.

(b)

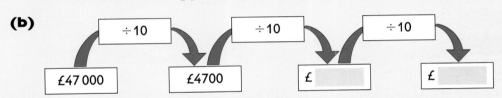

£47 000 → ÷10 → £4700 → ÷10 → £ → ÷10 → £

Describe what happens when numbers are divided by 10.

3 How many £10 notes are there in these amounts?

(a) £170 **(b)** £1700 **(c)** £17 000

4 School pencils are in packs of 10.
There are 10 packs in a box.
There are 10 boxes in a case.

(a) How many pencils are there
in a case?

One pencil costs 12p.

(b) How much does a case cost?

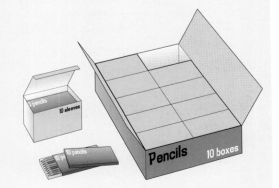

Large numbers

Space travellers Sean and Amanda are orbiting Jupiter.

Jupiter is
778 330 500 km
from the sun.

The sun
looks tiny from here!
How far is Jupiter from
the sun?

? **Amanda is thinking about this number.**
Answer her questions for her.

778 330 500
How many millions?
How many thousands?
What is left over?

Task

Copy and complete the table.
Read the distances and fill in the missing boxes.

Planet	Distance from sun	Number in words
Mercury	57 910 000 km	
Venus		One hundred and eight million, two hundred thousand kilometres
Earth	149 600 000 km	
Mars		Two hundred and twenty seven million, nine hundred and forty thousand kilometres
Saturn	1 429 400 000 km	One billion …

? **Look at the numbers in the table.**
Why are the digits grouped in threes?

? **Look at this number:** 17 203 385

Rearrange the digits to make the largest number possible.

Exercise

1 Match these number cards to the word cards.

| 4 823 407 | Four million, two hundred and eighty four thousand, three hundred and seven | 4 834 370 |

| Four million, eight hundred and thirty four thousand, three hundred and seventy | 4 284 307 | Four million, eight hundred and twenty three thousand, four hundred and seven |

2 Look at these number lines.
What numbers do the arrows point to?

(a)

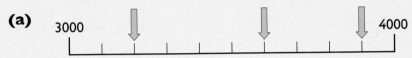

3000 ... 4000

(b)

60 000 ... 70 000

(c)

500 000 ... 600 000

(d)

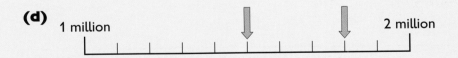

1 million ... 2 million

3 Put these numbers in order from the smallest to the largest.

(a) 3974, 7268, 1985, 999, 4900, 5002

(b) 12 592, 15 922, 12 295, 15 229, 19 252, 19 225

(c) 532 849, 290 110, 333 456, 345 336, 523 849, 291 100

4 Copy and complete this number sentence:
$38\,264 + \boxed{} = 78\,264$

The metric system

Jim Leggit wins 4 km Junior Road Race!

'Chorley Chase'

Cross country race over a distance of 5500 metres

All athletes welcome!

 Which race is longer?

 In the metric system 'kilo' stands for 1000. 1 kilometre is 1000 metres. How many grams are there in a kilogram?

 How many centimetres are there in a metre?
What does 'centi' mean?
What does 'milli' mean?
What does 'deci' mean?

Flapjacks

75 grams of sugar
75 grams of margarine
50 grams of golden syrup
150 grams of rolled oats
35 grams of dried fruit

Task

Look at this recipe.
It makes flapjacks for 12 people.

Copy and complete the table.
Show the weights in kilograms and grams.

	Party of 120		School of 1200		Army of 12 000	
Sugar		g	kg	g	kg	g
Margarine		g	kg	g	kg	g
Golden syrup		g	kg	g	kg	g
Oats	kg	g	kg	g	kg	g
Dried fruit		g	kg	g	kg	g

 Mark takes 5 ml of his medicine twice a day.
How long does his medicine last?

Medicine

500 ml

Exercise

1 Match each measurement in **List A** to the same measurement in **List B**.

List A

(a) 85 millilitres × 10
(b) 850 grams × 10
(c) 1400 cm
(d) 360 metres × 10
(e) 8500 g ÷ 10
(f) 360 centimetres

List B

(a) 140 cm × 10
(b) 36 cm × 10
(c) 85 g × 10
(d) 8500 ml ÷ 10
(e) 3600 m
(f) 85 g × 100

2 Look at this domino trail.
The right end of the green domino (**A**), matches the left end of the pink domino (**B**).

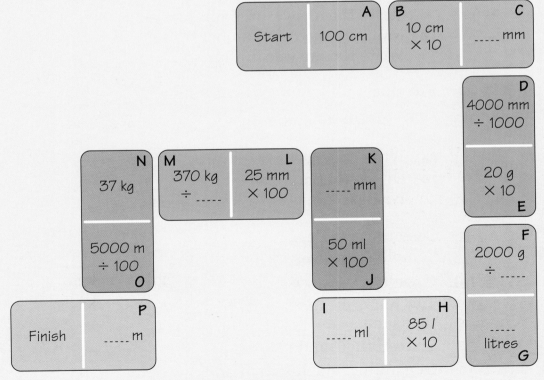

Complete the domino ends **C**, **F**, **G**, **I**, **K**, **M** and **P**.

Activity

  Make your own domino trail. Stick it down onto a poster.

Finishing off

- read whole numbers in figures and words
- understand what each digit represents
- multiply and divide whole numbers by 10, 100 or 1000
- order a set of numbers
- find a number which lies between two given numbers.

Review exercise

1 Put this number into your calculator.

> Six hundred and two thousand, nine hundred and forty

(a) Divide it by 10.
Write the answer in figures.
(b) Multiply the new number by 100.
Write the answer in words.

2 Put this number in your calculator.

> 20 975 000

(a) Write this number in words.
(b) Divide this number by 10.
Write the answer in words and figures.

3 Copy these tables.
Complete them using a calculator.

(a)

Number in words	÷10	÷10 again	÷10 again
Two hundred and twenty thousand			
Sixteen thousand			
One million one hundred and one thousand			

(b)

Number in words	×10	×10 again	×10 again
Twenty five			
Eight hundred and forty seven			
Nine thousand, nine hundred and nine			

4 Fill in the missing numbers on these number lines.

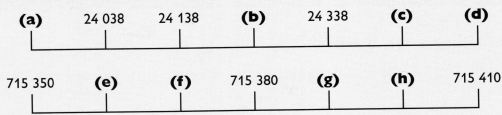

(a) 24 038   24 138   **(b)**   24 338   **(c)**   **(d)**

715 350   **(e)**   **(f)**   715 380   **(g)**   **(h)**   715 410

5 **(a)** Rearrange the digits in this number to make five new numbers.

24 778

(b) Put the five new numbers in order with the smallest first.

In the number 24 778, the **2** is worth twenty thousand.

(c) Write in words what the **4** is worth in each of your five numbers.

6 Look at these digits.

3, 6, 1, 8, 8, 4, 9

(a) What is the largest number you can make from these digits?
   Use each digit once.
   Write this number in figures and words.
(b) What is the smallest number you can make?
   Write this number in figures and words.

7 Look at this recipe for Party Punch.

Ingredients

2 litres of lemonade
450 ml orange juice
300 ml grapefruit juice
250 ml pineapple juice

It makes enough drink for 6 people.

(a) How many millilitres of drink are there?
(b) Write the recipe for 60 people.
(c) Each glass holds 250 ml.
   How many glasses does the original recipe make?

2 Position

Class 7G has a new teacher.
She draws a seating plan.

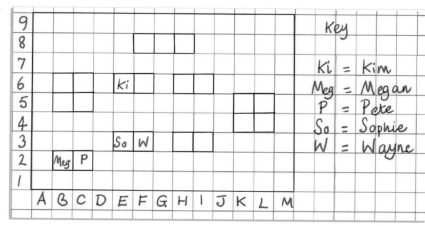

Pete sits in **column** C.

? **Which row does Pete sit in?**

? **Which position does Pete sit in?**

Samir sits in position **F6**.

Go along to F.   Then go up 6.

? **Who does Samir sit next to?**

Task

The other children sit in these seats:

John	**L4**	Alan	**I3**	Harry	**C5**	Tim	**B5**	Karl	**K4**
Mercy	**B6**	Humza	**H6**	Lucy	**H8**	Andy	**F8**	Christina	**K5**
Jo	**G8**	Jack	**I6**	Ali	**L5**	Meena	**C6**	Michelle	**H3**

1 Copy and complete the teacher's seating plan using this information.

2 On squared paper, draw a seating plan for **your** classroom.
Make a list of all the people in the class, and give their **positions**.

? **How are aeroplane seats numbered?**

Exercise

This is a map of Mr Mac's farm.

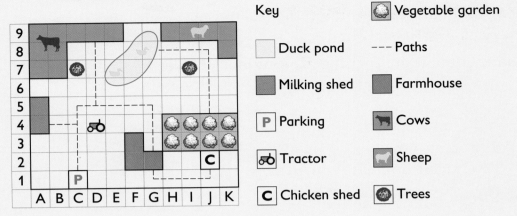

Key

 Vegetable garden

☐ Duck pond   --- Paths

▨ Milking shed   ▨ Farmhouse

P Parking   🐄 Cows

🚜 Tractor   🐑 Sheep

C Chicken shed   ⊛ Trees

Class 7G are visiting the farm.
They use the map to find their way around.

I   The teacher asks these questions.

> *(a)* *Where do we park the bus?*
> *(b)* *In which squares are the sheep?*
> *(c)* *What is in square H4?*
> *(d)* *Where is the chicken shed?*
> *(e)* *What will you see in these squares: F7, G2, C7, D4?*

These are Alan's answers.

(a) G7
(b) H9, I9, J9, K9, K8
(c) Chickens
(d) J2
(e) F7 tractor, G2 tree, C7 ducks, D4 farmhouse

Some of Alan's answers are wrong.
How can you tell?
What are the correct answers?

2   Mrs Mac makes a special cream tea for the class.
The class walk from the milking shed to the farmhouse for tea.

Which squares do they walk through? (Keep to the paths!)

Activity   Find out how to play 'Starships'.

SU   Play the game with a friend.

Directions

The four main directions on a compass are:
North, **E**ast, **S**outh and **W**est.

Remember the order. Turning **clockwise**: **N**ever
Ever
Support
Wolves!

? **What does clockwise mean?**
What is the opposite of clockwise?

Task

This is a map of a maze.

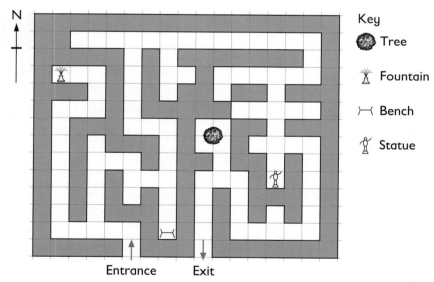

Key
🌳 Tree
⛲ Fountain
⊢⊣ Bench
👤 Statue

I Where do these instructions lead?

From the **statue**, 2 paces north, 2 paces east, 5 paces south,
4 paces west, 3 paces north, 2 paces west, 4 paces south.

2 Write instructions to walk from the **entrance** to somewhere else in the maze.
You can only give instructions using the four compass directions and the
number of paces.

Swap instructions with a friend and test each other.

The direction between **north** and **west** is called **north-west**.

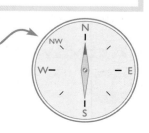

? **What are the other three directions called?**

Exercise

1 Look at this map.

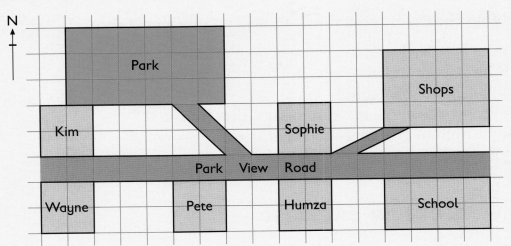

(a) Who lives north of Wayne?

(b) Who lives south of Sophie?

(c) What is east of Humza's house?

(d) Kim's best friend lives in the house to the west of Pete. Who is Kim's best friend?

(e) Humza walks to the park. In which direction does he go?

(f) Sophie is the same age as the person who lives south-west of her. Who is the same age as Sophie?

Activity

SU

In this computer game, you are Zapman ( ).

Zap the Blobs ( ) by landing on their squares.

Each square you go through makes you weaker, but landing on a burger ( ) makes you strong again.

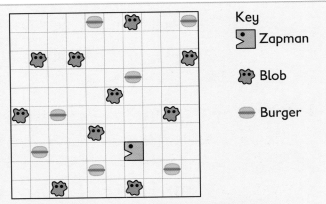

Key

 Zapman

 Blob

 Burger

If you go through 5 squares without zapping a Blob or eating a burger you lose.

Help Zapman by giving him instructions.

You can move forwards (↑), backwards (↓), left (←) or right (→).

For example, to move Zapman forward 3 squares, write ↑3.

How many Blobs can you zap?

Finishing off

Now that you have finished this chapter you should:

- be able to describe a square on a grid
- be able to understand simple seating plans
- be able to use simple maps
- know the eight main compass directions
- be able to give directions using compass points.

Review exercise

1 **(a)** Use the letter square to find out what these messages say. The first word has been done for you.

	A	B	C	D	E	F	G	H
8	a	c	r	j	b	w	k	g
7	j	z	v	h	b	f	y	h
6	o	n	a	g	s	u	a	o
5	q	g	b	j	p	l	x	e
4	l	y	f	k	d	f	v	c
3	s	i	e	t	i	c	z	p
2	w	q	n	e	k	x	d	m
1	d	i	l	m	r	t	u	h

(i) H2, C3, C3, F1 / D1, H5 / A8, D3 /
   M e e t
   F1, D7, C3 / E6, H1, A6, E5, E6.

(ii) D1, G6, D3, H7, A3 / B3, E6 / F3, H6, A6, F5!

(iii) F3, A6, D1, C3 / D3, A6 / H2, G7 /
   E5, A8, E1, D3, B4.

(iv) D1, G7 / E4, A6, H8 / B1, E6 /
   B8, C6, C1, F5, H5, E4 / H2, G6, F2.

(b) Use the letter square to write your own message.
   Give the message to a friend to solve.

2 This grid is used for a game of noughts and crosses. Ali and Jo had these goes.

Jo wins the game.
Where did she put her O?

| Ali (X) | A3, A1, C1. |
| Jo (O) | B2, A2. |

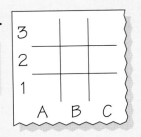

3 This is a spreadsheet from a computer screen.

	A	B	C	D	E	F	G
1	Day	vanilla	chocolate	raspberry	strawberry	totals	
2							
3							
4	Monday	18	23	10	12	63	
5	Tuesday	20	20	8	15		
6	Wednesday	13	5	2	4		
7	Thursday	25	25	18	17		
8	Friday	40	32	20	36		
9							
10	totals	116	105				
11							

F4 = =SUM(B4:E4)

Ice cream sales in one week.xls

The spreadsheet shows how many ice creams a shop sold last week. Each rectangle is called a **cell**.

(a) What number is in cell D5?

(b) Which cell shows the number of raspberry ice creams sold on Thursday?

(c) Why does 'F4' appear above the grid?

Look above the grid. You can see the instruction =SUM(B4:E4)

This means 'add all the numbers from cells B4 to E4 together'.

(d) How many ice creams were sold altogether on Monday?

(e) Cell E10 is for the total number of strawberry ice creams. What instruction do you type in cell E10?

Activity   On the computer, copy the spreadsheet and complete all the totals.

Addition

Harry is practising snooker.

> Rule for potting: red, colour, red, colour, red …
>   until a ball does not go in. This is called a **break**.
>
> Rules of scoring: ●7, ○6, ●5, ●4, ●3, ○2, ●1.

? **What is Harry's score for this break?**

Red,   black,   red,   blue
 ●   ●   ●   ●

  1   +   7   + ⬜ + ⬜ = ⬜

Harry already has a score of 37.
He works out his new total.

    37
  + 14
  ———
    51

? **Explain Harry's working.**

Task

Harry and Megan play a game of snooker.
Copy and complete the table.

Harry				Megan			
Break		**Break score**	**Total**	**Break**		**Break score**	**Total**
●●●●●				●●●●●●			
●●●●				●●●●●●			
●●●○				●●●●			

When there are no more reds left, the colours are potted in order.

> When potting colours in order, the colours stay in the pocket and
> cannot be repeated.

? **What is the largest possible break in a game?**

Exercise

1 Pick out 5 pairs of numbers that add up to 10.

3 2 6 5 9 1 7 5 4 8

2 Pick out 5 pairs of numbers that add up to 30.

12 17 9 25 11 18 13 21 19 5

3 Pick out 5 pairs of numbers that add up to 50.

39 22 27 37 46 28 11 13 23 4

4 Meena and Sophie go on holiday in a car.

(a) Work out how far they travel each day.

	Monday	Tuesday	Wednesday	Thursday	Friday
Morning	96 km	132 km	128 km	103 km	127 km
Afternoon	80 km	86 km	77 km	98 km	85 km

(b) How far do they travel altogether?

su

5 Copy these bricks and fill in the spaces.
Here is an example.

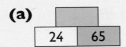

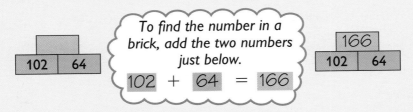

To find the number in a brick, add the two numbers just below.

102 + 64 = 166

(a)

24 65

(b)

73 54

(c)

521 456

(d)

23 37 58

(e)

384 297 512

(f)

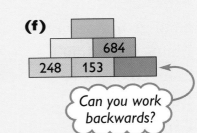

684

248 153

Can you work backwards?

Subtraction

Kim and Lucy are visiting Kim's Grandma.
It is a 240 mile journey.
They set the trip meter to zero at the start.

When they join the motorway, Kim works out how far they still have to go.

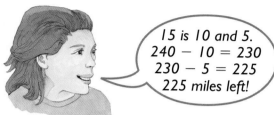

15 is 10 and 5.
240 − 10 = 230
230 − 5 = 225
225 miles left!

Kim

 015

? **Explain what Kim has done.**

Later Lucy writes down

076

$$\begin{array}{r} 2\overset{1}{\cancel{4}}\overset{3}{\cancel{1}}0 \\ -\ \ 76 \\ \hline 164 \end{array}$$

164 miles left!

Lucy

? **Explain what Lucy has done.**

Task

Copy and complete this record of Kim and Lucy's journey.

Place	Meter (miles covered)	Miles still to go
Home	000	240
Join motorway	015	225
Stop for petrol	076	164
Change motorway	103	
Stop for lunch	135	
Stuck in traffic	159	
Change motorway	178	
Phone Grandma	213	
Leave motorway	222	
Reach Grandma's town	237	
Arrive	240	

? **How do you work out 202 − 195?**

Exercise

1 John is collecting money for new shirts for his football team.
They cost £154.
How much more does he need when he has

(a) £42   **(b)** £72   **(c)** £93   **(d)** £124   **(e)** £153?

2 Copy the crossword grid.
Fill in the answers with one digit in each square.

	1	2		
3				4
5			6	
		7		
	8			

Across
1 638 − 200
5 303 − 287
6 418 − 328
8 953 − 432

Down
2 734 − 699
3 1000 − 784
4 850 − 46
7 615 − 583

3 India have a score of 218 runs.
England are batting. They have 176 runs.
How many more do they need   **(a)** to draw level   **(b)** to win?

4 Michelle takes €350 (350 euros)
spending money on holiday.

(a) She spends €22 on a meal.
How much has she left?

(b) Then she spends €127
on an outing.
How much is left now?

(c) She buys a dress for €98.
How much is left now?

(d) She also buys some
perfume for €59.
How much is left?

(e) A scarf costs €45.
Can she afford it?

Multiplication

John is playing darts.
3 darts are thrown in one turn.
Then the scores are added together.

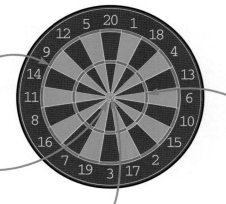

The outer ring is double.

The inner ring is treble.

This is 25.

John gets   treble 7   and 3   and double 15

This is the bull. it is double 25, so 50.

? **How many does John score?**

Task

I What is the total score for

(a) double 6   **(b)** double 14   **(c)** treble 6

(d)    **(e)**    **(f)**

(g) double 4 and treble 2   **(h)** double 12 and treble 2   **(i)** treble 18 and 6?

2 (a) John scores 71 from 3 darts. He gets a treble and a double.
Copy and complete his calculation.

	1st dart	2nd dart (treble)	3rd dart (double)	
Number	10	7		
Score		+	+	= 71

(b) Work out how John could get   **(i)** 69   **(ii)** 14   from 3 darts.
One is a double and one is a treble.

? **How do you work out 6 × 231?**

Exercise

1 Work out these.

(a) (i) 3×4 (ii) 3×40 (iii) 3×400

(b) (i) 5×7 (ii) 5×70 (iii) 5×700

(c) (i) 6×8 (ii) 60×8 (iii) 600×8

(d) (i) 7×9 (ii) 70×9 (iii) 700×9

2 Copy and complete these.

(a) $2 \times 7 = \boxed{}$ (b) $\boxed{} \times 6 = 48$ (c) $4 \times \boxed{} = 36$ (d) $8 \times 9 = \boxed{}$

(e) $\boxed{} \times 6 = 72$ (f) $7 \times \boxed{} = 56$ (g) $6 \times \boxed{} = 18$ (h) $\boxed{} \times 6 = 0$

3 In the picture you can see 1 cluster of balloons. There are 6 clusters of balloons on a table. How many balloons are there altogether?

4 Many things are sold in packs.

(a) How many videos are there in (i) 4 packs (ii) 5 packs?

Videos Packs of 3

(b) How many boxes are there in (i) 3 packs (ii) 8 packs?

Cereal 8 boxes

(c) How many cards are there in (i) 7 packs (ii) 9 packs?

Greetings cards: packs of 6

(d) How many treats are there in (i) 5 packs (ii) 14 packs?

12 dog treats

Chocosticks

5 Six friends go out together in Paris. Find the total cost of

(a) their meal
(b) their tickets to the theatre
(c) their ice-cream.

Menu €23

Theatre €28

€2

6 A coach trip costs £65 per person. How much does a trip for a family of 3 people cost altogether?

Division

A group of seven friends go on a holiday.
They share all the costs.

Christina buys coffee and muffins for £7.35.
She writes:

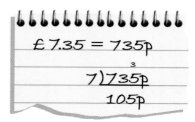

£7.35 = 735p

$7)\overline{735p}$
     105p

That is £1.05 each.

Christina

? **Explain the steps of Christina's working.**

Task

Copy and complete the sheet of expenses for the friends' holiday.

Item	Cost	Paid by	Amount each
Coffee and muffins	£7.35	Christina	£1.05
Van hire	£140.00	Sophie	
Picnic	£22.40	Lucy	
Entrance to castle	£53.20	Samir	
Car park for beach	£5.25	Sophie	
Swimming baths	£	Jack	£2.80
Restaurant meal	£86.45	Mercy	£12.45
Entrance to aquarium	£31.50	Pete	
Disco	£	Jack	£2.30
		Total	

Is this correct?

? **How do you share £1 between 7 people?**

Exercise

1 Work out these.

(a) $24 \div 8 = \boxed{}$ (b) $64 \div \boxed{} = 8$ (c) $36 \div 9 = \boxed{}$

(d) $\boxed{} \div 9 = 1$ (e) $48 \div \boxed{} = 6$ (f) $\boxed{} \div 7 = 8$

(g) $\boxed{} \div 9 = 9$ (h) $45 \div \boxed{} = 9$ (i) $72 \div \boxed{} = 9$

2 (a) Which of these are even numbers?

     592   713   834   1055   1068

(b) Divide all your answers to part (a) by 2.

(c) Can you divide any of these by 2 again?

3 (a) Which of these can you divide exactly by 5?

     105   815   1023   1040   2319

(b) Divide your answers to part (a) by 5.

4 (a) Work out the answers to these questions.

(i) $42 \div 3$ (ii) $350 \div 7$ (iii) $108 \div 12$

(iv) $456 \div 8$ (v) $42 \div 7$ (vi) $280 \div 8$

(vii) $92 \div 2$ (viii) $63 \div 9$ (ix) $198 \div 9$

(x) $60 \div 3$ (xi) $240 \div 5$ (xii) $96 \div 8$

(xiii) $138 \div 6$ (xiv) $132 \div 3$ (xv) $371 \div 7$

(xvi) $36 \div 18$ (xvii) $208 \div 8$

(b) Trace this picture and shade with one colour the regions containing your answers.

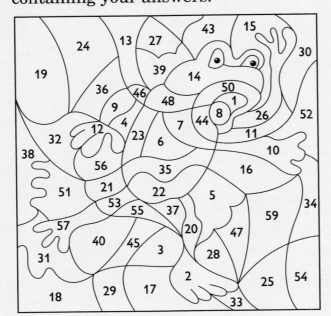

SU

Finishing off

Now that you have finished this chapter you should be able to:

- add whole numbers
- multiply whole numbers
- subtract whole numbers
- divide whole numbers.

Review exercise

1 Four friends are playing darts. The scores are given below.

(a) Find the total score for each player.

(i) Jo	12	**(ii)** Alan Double 12
	Treble 18	Treble 19
	2	16

(iii) Kim Treble 18   **(iv)** Karl Double 7
Treble 19   Double 14
Double 10   Treble 6

(b) Who has the highest score?

2 Mark buys some items.
Each time he pays with a 50p coin.
How much change does he get each time?

(a) Pencil sharpener 37p
(b) Postage stamp   41p
(c) Newspaper   35p
(d) Apple   13p

3 Teams score 3 points for winning a match, 1 point for a draw, 0 points for losing.
Find the total points scored by

(a) Shellbury   6 wins
(b) Eastpool   5 wins and 1 draw
(c) Churchton   6 draws
(d) Avonford   2 wins, 3 draws and 1 loss.

4 Humza has 4 pieces of wood, each 1 m long.
He cuts these lengths off them.
What lengths remain?

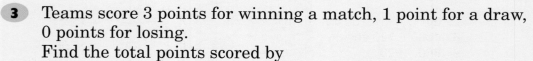

1 metre = 1000 millimetres.

(a) 970 mm   (b) 420 mm   (c) 235 mm   (d) 815 mm

5 In the card game Bridge, cards are worth these points.

Ace
4 points

King
3 points

Queen
2 points

Jack
1 point

Work out the total point value for these cards.
(a) 3 Aces and 1 King
(b) 2 Kings, 3 Queens and a Jack
(c) 1 Ace, 2 Kings and 2 Queens
(d) 3 Aces, 3 Kings, 4 Queens and 2 Jacks

SU

6 Copy the crossword grid below. Fill in your answers to the clues.

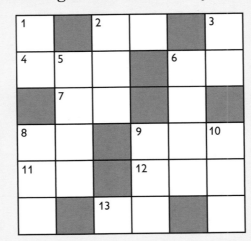

Across

2 3×13
4 6×31
6 $140 \div 5$
7 $20 + 18 + 4$ and divide the answer by 3
8 $1000 - 720$ and divide the answer by 7
9 $660 - 229$
11 7×7
12 $1000 - 177$
13 3×19

Down

1 $43 + 18$
2 $1456 \div 4$
3 6×3
5 $6201 + 857 + 1051$
6 $2828 + 4$
8 $2 \times 2 \times 2 \times 5 \times 11$
9 $4 \times 8 \times 15$ and then add 7
10 11×12

Activity Time yourself for this question.

(a) $736 + 203 =$ ☐   **(b)** $14 + 23 + 17 =$ ☐   **(c)** $99 + 98 =$ ☐

(d) $230 - 96 =$ ☐   **(e)** $300 - 97 =$ ☐   **(f)** $180 - 153 =$ ☐

(g) ☐ $\times 7 = 56$ **(h)** $421 \times 7 =$ ☐   **(i)** $72 \div$ ☐ $= 8$

(j) $324 \div 9 =$ ☐   **(k)** $6 \times 12 =$ ☐   **(l)** $7 \times 7 =$ ☐

How long did it take you to get them **all** right?

4 Angles

The angle at the corner of a square is called a **right angle**.

 Where can you see right angles in your classroom?

Types of angle

Acute angle

Smaller than a right angle.

Obtuse angle

Bigger than a right angle.

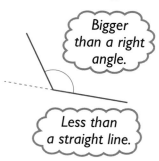

Less than a straight line.

Reflex angle

Bigger than a straight line.

Task

Work with a friend.

1 One person places their hand on a piece of paper. The other person draws round it.

2 Draw lines to show the angles between the fingers.

 (a) Which fingers have the largest angle between them?

 (b) Which fingers have the smallest angle between them?

 (c) What type of angles have you drawn?

3 Can you make an obtuse angle with your finger and thumb?
 Draw round a hand that makes an obtuse angle.
 Draw lines to show the obtuse angle.

Keep your drawings for the next lesson.

Angle.

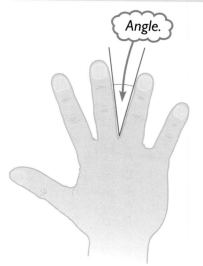

 Can you open your arms to make a reflex angle?

 Explain the word 'angle' to a Martian.

Exercise

1 Write these angles in order of size, smallest first.

2 Look at the angles below.
Which angles are **(a)** acute **(b)** obtuse **(c)** reflex?

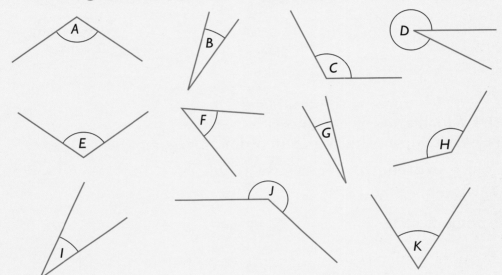

3 **(a)** How many right angles make angle *X*?

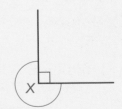

(b) How many right angles make a **whole turn**?

Whole turn.

4 Draw and label
   (a) an obtuse angle
   (b) a reflex angle
   (c) an acute angle.

5 How many right angles can you see
in this shape?

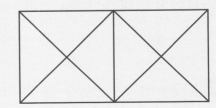

Measuring angles

Task

1 Look at the angles.

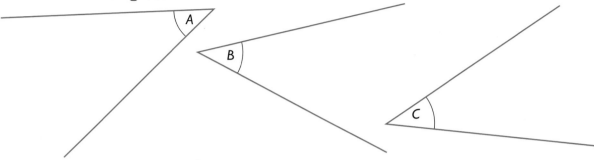

(a) Which angle is the smallest?
(b) Which angle is the largest?
(c) Write down the angles in order of size, smallest first.

You use a **protractor** to measure angles.

Angles are measured in **degrees**.

This angle is 42°.

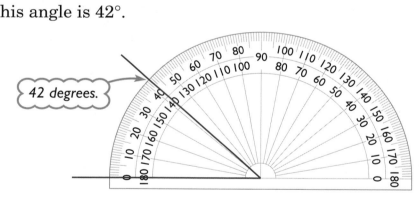

42 degrees.

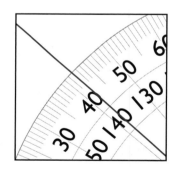

? **Why are there two scales on the protractor?**
How do you know which scale to use?

2 Use a protractor to measure the angles in part 1.
Were your answers in part 1 correct?

3 Find the finger angles you drew last lesson.
Use a protractor to measure the angles.

? **How many degrees are there**
(a) in a right angle **(b) on a straight line** **(c) in a whole turn?**

Exercise

1 Here are five angles.

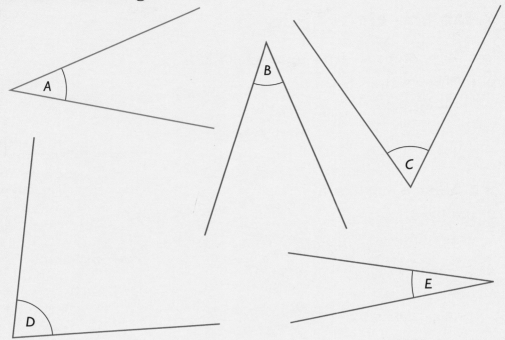

Here are the sizes of the angles **in the wrong order**.

60°   40°   20°   35°   80°

Measure the angles.
Which angle is which size?

Investigation

1 How many straight lines are drawn to make this star?

2 Measure the angles at the points of this star.

3 Add up the five angles.

4 Draw two different five-pointed stars.
Use five lines for each, like this one.
Add up the angles for each star.

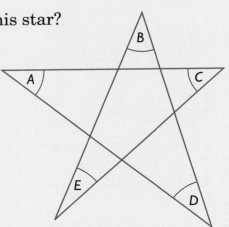

? What do you notice each time?

5 Repeat this investigation with seven-pointed stars.

Drawing angles

" Do the right thing!

Follow these steps to draw an angle of 57°.

Step 1 Draw a line.
Make a mark near one end.

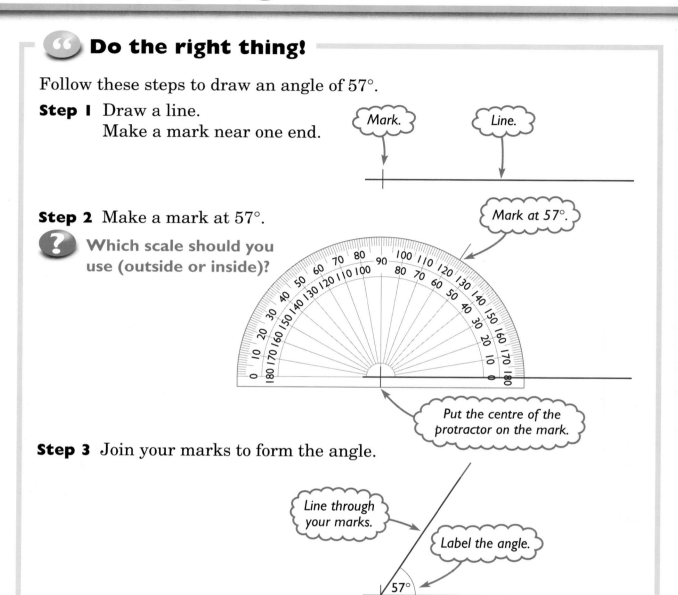

Step 2 Make a mark at 57°.

? **Which scale should you use (outside or inside)?**

Mark.

Line.

Mark at 57°.

Put the centre of the protractor on the mark.

Step 3 Join your marks to form the angle.

Line through your marks.

Label the angle.

57°

Task

Use a protractor to draw these wheel spokes.
There are nine spokes.
All the angles should be 40°.

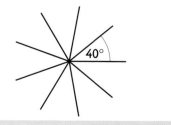

40°

? **How do you draw a right angle?**
Do you need a protractor to draw an angle of 180°?

Exercise

1 Follow the three steps to draw each of these angles.
Make sure you are neat and accurate.

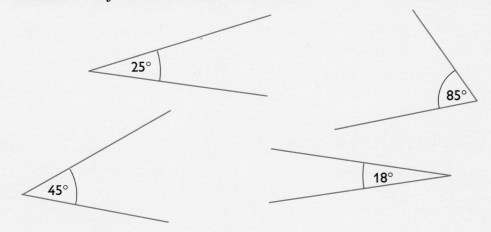

25°

85°

45°

18°

2 Draw these angles.
   (a) 75°   **(b)** 35°   **(c)** 47°   **(d)** 10°

Investigation

Look at your protractor.
60° and 120° are on the same line.
60° + 120° = 180°.

Choose five other pairs like this.
Add each pair.
What do you notice? Explain your answer.

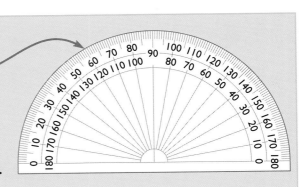

Activity

1 Draw an angle of 120°.

? Is 120° acute, obtuse or reflex?

2 Draw an angle of 140°.
3 Draw an angle of 165°.

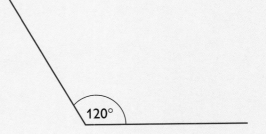

120°

Finishing off

Now that you have finished this chapter you should know:
• that a whole turn is 360°, a straight line is 180°, and a right angle is 90° • what the words **acute**, **obtuse** and **reflex** mean • how to use a protractor to measure and draw angles.

Review exercise

1 **(a)** Write down these angles in order of size, largest first.

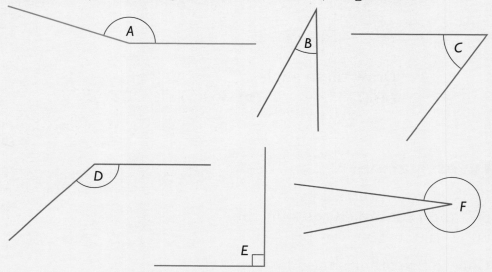

(b) Which of the above angles are
(i) obtuse **(ii)** reflex **(iii)** acute?

2 Measure these angles with your protractor.
Measure them as accurately as you can.

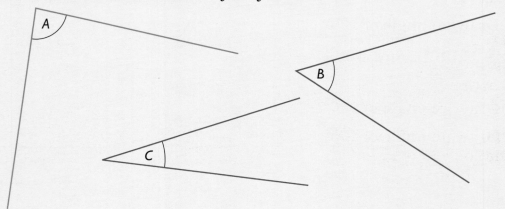

3 Make accurate drawings of these angles and label them.

(a)

30°

(b)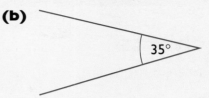

35°

4 How many right angles are there

(a) on a straight line
(b) in a whole turn
(c) in 270°?

5 How many degrees are there

(a) in a right angle
(b) in a whole turn?

6 Write down these angles in order of size, smallest first.

| 53° | An obtuse angle | A right angle |

| 300° | A straight line | 240° | 3° |

7 Draw and label these angles.

(a) The corner of a square
(b) 110°

8 Make an accurate drawing of a rectangle.

Investigation

Draw a large triangle.
Measure the angles inside it.
Add up the three angles.

Repeat this for two other triangles.
What do you notice?

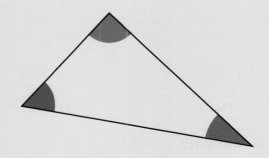

5 Displaying data

Tally charts

Class 7G are on an outing.

Mr Jones

An ice cream for everyone. Say what flavour you want.

Strawberry	Chocolate	Raspberry ripple	Mint choc chip	Strawberry
Vanilla	Strawberry	Mint choc chip	Chocolate	Strawberry
Mint choc chip	Vanilla	Chocolate	Strawberry	Vanilla
Mint choc chip	Strawberry	Raspberry ripple	Raspberry ripple	Chocolate
Chocolate	Strawberry			

Task

Mr Jones makes a tally chart.

Flavour	Tally	Frequency
Strawberry	ⵜ‖‖ ‖	7
Chocolate		
Vanilla		
Mint choc chip		
Raspberry ripple		
	Total	

Frequency means the number for this flavour.

 What does ⵜ‖‖ mean?

Copy and complete the tally chart.

Find the total. How does this check your work?

 You can find the most popular flavour from the tally chart. How?

 Which is more useful, the list of flavours or the tally chart. Why?

 How many ice creams does Mr Jones buy?
Which number in the tally chart tells you this?

Exercise

SU

1 This tally chart shows the type of birds visiting a bird table.

Type of bird	Tally	Frequency
Starling	ⵑ‖‖	
Blackbird	ⵑⵑ ‖	
Robin	‖‖	
Blue tit	‖	
Chaffinch	ⵑ ‖‖‖	
	Total	

(a) Copy the table and complete the frequency column.
(b) What is the most common type of bird?
(c) How many birds visited the bird table?

SU

2 Christina wants to know the favourite sport of the children in her class.
She writes a list of their favourite sports.

hockey	netball	football	football	tennis	football
hockey	swimming	swimming	tennis	tennis	football
tennis	football	cricket	football	football	tennis
netball	cricket	swimming	swimming	netball	tennis

(a) Copy and complete the tally chart.
(b) What is the favourite sport?
(c) How many children are in the class?

Sport	Tally	Frequency
Hockey		
Netball		

SU

3 Mark throws a die 24 times.
He thinks it is hardest to throw a 6.
Here are Mark's results.

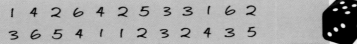

1 4 2 6 4 2 5 3 3 1 6 2
3 6 5 4 1 1 2 3 2 4 3 5

(a) Draw a tally chart to show Mark's results.
It should start like this.

Number on die	Tally	Frequency
1		

(b) Do you agree with Mark?

Bar charts and pictograms

Pete asks his class about their favourite music.
The bar chart shows the results.

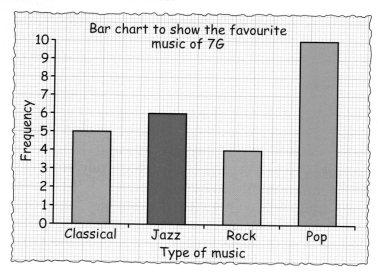

 What does the word frequency mean?

How many children like rock music?
How do you know this from the bar chart?

Task

Pete decides to show his data in a pictogram as well.
First he fills in the 'Classical' row.

Classical	♪ ♪ ♪ ♪ ♪
Jazz	
Rock	
Pop	

1 Copy and complete the pictogram on squared paper.

2 Find out the favourite music of everyone in your class.
Display your results on a bar chart and a pictogram.

3 Compare your results with Pete's class.

Which do you like better, a bar chart or a pictogram? Why?

Exercise

1 Mrs Brown owns a sweet shop.
She keeps a record of the chocolate bars she sells one day.

Chocolate	Frequency
Snackers	8
Krispin	10
Peanut crisp	5
Choco bar	9
Tiger bar	7

Draw a bar chart to show this information.
Make sure your bar chart has

(a) a title

(b) a label for each bar

(c) a scale to show frequency.

2

There are too many cars on the road. People should share cars.

Tim

Tim counts the number of people in each car passing his school.

Number of people in car	Number of cars
1	20
2	15
3	8
4	5
5	3

(a) Draw a bar chart to show the results of Tim's survey.

(b) Draw a pictogram to show the results of Tim's survey.

Use a for each car.

Tim makes a poster to show his results.

(c) Which will look better, the bar chart or the pictogram?

Activity Do a survey to find out how the pupils in your class come to school.
Make a poster to show the results of your survey.

Pie charts

Look at this pie chart.

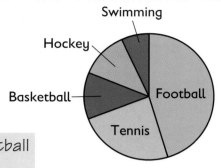

Football is the most popular sport.

More people like basketball than swimming.

More than half like football.

Hockey is the least popular.

About a quarter like tennis.

? Some of these comments are true, others are false.
Which are true, which are false?

Task

Michelle has counted how many sweets of each colour are in this tube.

Red 12   Green 9   Blue 6   Pink 6   Yellow 3

Michelle has started to draw a pie chart.

36 sweets means 10° for one sweet.

Michelle

Sweets

? Explain what Michelle says.

1 Why has she used an angle of 90° to show green?
2 What angle is needed to show red?
3 Copy and complete the pie chart for Michelle.

Michelle has drawn this bar chart to show the colours of sweets.

? Is it the same tube of sweets?

? Which shows the information better, the pie chart or the bar chart?

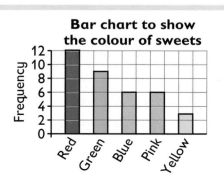

Bar chart to show the colour of sweets

Exercise

1 Harry has drawn a pie chart to show how he spends his pocket money.

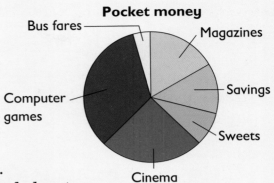

Pocket money

(a) What does he spend most money on?

(b) List the items in the pie chart in order of the amount he spends on them. Start with the thing he spends least on.

2 This pie chart and bar chart show the same data.

The sale of drinks in Annie's café

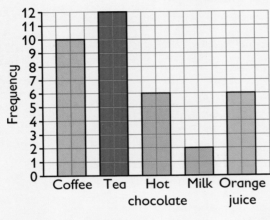

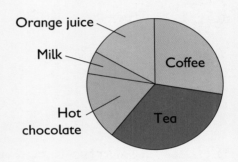

For each question below

(i) find the answer

(ii) say where you can find the answer, bar chart, pie chart or both.

(a) Which is the most popular drink?

(b) Two drinks together give half the sales. Which are they?

(c) How many hot chocolates are sold?

(d) Which two drinks have the same sales?

Activity This table shows the pets of Megan's friends.

Draw a pie chart and a bar chart to show this.

Make a poster.

Pet	Frequency
Dog	3
Cat	6
Pony	2
Hamster	1

Finishing off

Now that you have finished this chapter you should be able to:

● use a tally chart to record data
● draw bar charts and pictograms
● understand pie charts.

Review exercise

1 Mrs Brown is buying sandwiches.
Draw a tally chart to show how many of each
type of sandwich she orders.

Sandwich menu
(all £2.50)
Beef
Chicken
Cheese
Ham
Prawn
Salad

beef	chicken	chicken	cheese	prawn
ham	ham	salad	chicken	prawn
ham	beef	ham	salad	cheese
prawn	ham	cheese	beef	ham
ham				

2 Mercy is making this design in patchwork.
Draw a tally chart to show how many squares of each colour
she needs.

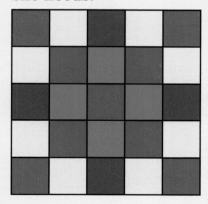

3 A tennis club are voting for a team captain.
Here are the results.

Name	Alan	Bethan	David	Gillian	Martin
Number of votes	10	8	12	2	6

(a) Draw a bar chart to show the result of the voting.

(b) How many people voted?

4 Mr Jones has written the name of each child in his class against the month of their birthday.

January	Wayne	Jo			
February	Andy	Pete	Megan		
March	Ali				
April	George	Sophie	Samir		
May	Meena	Saul	Alan		
June	Jack	Humza	Victoria	Zak	Lucy
July	Mark	Karl			
August					
September	Ahmed	Tim			
October	Harry	Mercy	Christina	John	
November	Michelle				
December	Sally	Ginny	Kim		

(a) Which month has most birthdays?

(b) Draw a bar chart to show these data.

5 The pie chart shows the type of weather in Avonford last June.

Weather in June

Avonford Star

Avonford enjoys a sunny June!

(a) Look carefully at the pie chart.
Do you agree with the newspaper headline?
Give a reason for your answer.

(b) Write down 2 things that the pie chart tells you about the weather last June.

Activity Collect some data of your own.
Use a tally chart and a frequency table to record your data.
Display your data on a bar chart or pictogram.
Make a poster to show what you have found from your data.

Suggestions
Shoe sizes of your class.   The colours of cars in the car park.
Favourite football team.   The pets owned by children in your class.

Mrs Shah

Have you been working hard?

Yes!

Alan

Very hard.

Meena

Class 7G are playing some Maths games.
It is a reward for their hard work.

Money grabber

Meena and Alan are playing **Money grabber**.

Each of them starts with an 8 × 8 grid and a set of pretend coins.
Alan and Meena cannot see each other's grids.

Meena sets her grid up like this.

	A	B	C	D	E	F	G	H
8	1p							£2
7								
6					£1			
5								
4		5p				10p		
3			20p					
2							50p	
1		2p						

Alan starts.

Have you got a coin on H5?

? **What does Meena answer?**

Now it is Meena's turn.

Alan, I think you have a coin on A5.

No, I have not.

Now it is Alan's go again.

H8.

? **What does Meena say?**

Alan has got Meena's £2 coin. He banks it and his own £2 coin.
The game ends when there are no coins on the grids. The players have banked them all.

Alan

(£2) (£2) (20p) (20p) (5p) (5p) (2p) (2p)

Meena

(£1) (£1) (50p) (50p) (10p) (10p) (1p) (1p)

? **Who has won the game?**

We will play 10 games and add our scores together.

Task

Play **Money grabber** with a friend. Play 10 games.
The winner has the larger total.

Reflection

This is the flag of Japan.

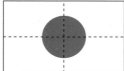

 What shape is the flag?

 What shape is in the middle of the flag?

 What happens when you put a mirror along the dotted lines?

The flag has **reflection symmetry**.

It has **two lines of symmetry**.

> *A line of symmetry can also be called a mirror line or an axis of symmetry.*

Task

I Draw and colour these flags to look like this.

Macedonia

Bahamas

Pakistan

Germany

South Africa

Switzerland

United Kingdom

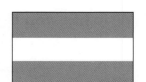
Austria

2 Draw all the lines of symmetry on each flag.

This is the Jamaican flag.

 What are the lines from corner to corner called?

 What happens when you put a mirror along these lines?

Exercise

1 **(a)** What is the name of each of these shapes?

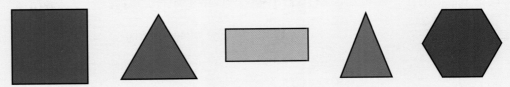

(b) Copy or trace the shapes.
Draw all their lines of symmetry.
How many lines of symmetry does each shape have?

2 How many lines of symmetry does each leaf or flower have?

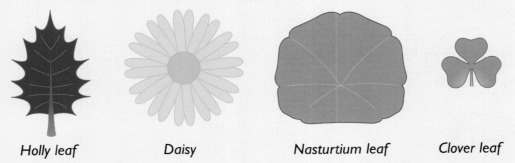

Holly leaf   Daisy   Nasturtium leaf   Clover leaf

3 This is a drawing of Mark's house.

(a) How many lines of symmetry does it have?

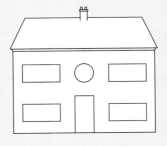

This is Mark's house after it was painted.

(b) How many lines of symmetry does it have now?

Activity On squared paper, design and colour a flag that has one line of symmetry.

Draw the line of symmetry first to help you.

Completing shapes

Jo is designing a cross stitch picture of a butterfly.

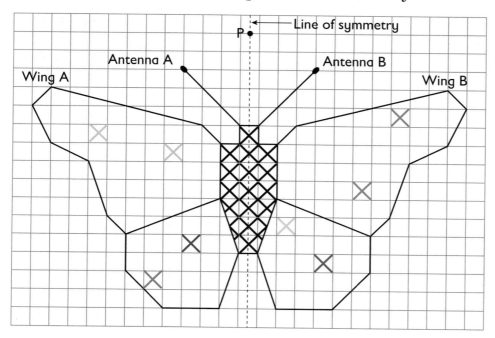

When it is finished, the design must have reflection symmetry.

Task

1 Use a ruler to measure from P (on the line of symmetry) to the tip of wing A.
Measure from P to the tip of wing B. Give your answers in mm.

What do you notice?

2 Measure from P to the tip of antenna A.
Measure from P to the tip of antenna B.

What do you notice?

3 Copy the design. Use the same colours as Jo.

Colour in eight more stitches to make the pattern symmetrical.

4 Colour in more stitches to complete Jo's design.

Make sure that it is symmetrical.

 Does Wayne have a line of symmetry?

Exercise

1 Each of these road signs has a line of symmetry.
The dotted line is the line of symmetry.

(a) Copy and complete each road sign by making it symmetrical.

(i) 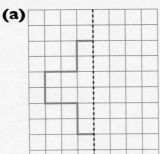 **(ii)** 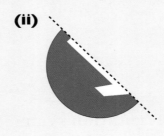 **(iii)**

(b) Find out what the road signs mean.

2 Copy and complete each symmetrical shape.

(a) **(b)** 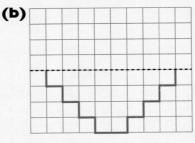 **(c)**

3 This sports club logo has two lines of symmetry.

Complete the design by colouring it correctly.

The letters have all been put in for you.

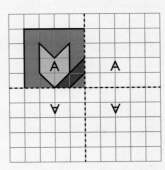

Activity On squared paper, design and colour a cross stitch pattern which has **two lines of symmetry**.

Draw the lines of symmetry first, to help you with your design.

Rotation

Look at these two cards.

? **Does the Ace of Diamonds look the same if it is upside down?**

? **What about the Ace of Hearts?**

The Ace of Diamonds has **rotation symmetry of order 2**.

? **What does this mean?**

Task

Look at these cards.

? **Which cards have rotation symmetry? How do you decide?**

Test each card.

Trace the cards onto paper and stick them into your book.
Write down the order of rotation symmetry of each card.

? **Where is the centre of rotation symmetry for each card?**

? **What is the order of rotation symmetry of these shapes?**

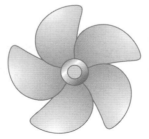

Exercise

1 Trace each of these shapes carefully.

(i)

(ii)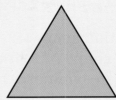

(iii)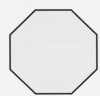

(iv)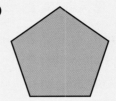

(a) Write down the name of each shape.

(b) Write down the order of rotation symmetry of each shape.

(c) Stick the shapes into your book.
Mark the centre of rotation of each shape with a cross.

2 These are car hub caps.

(i)

(ii)

(iii)

(a) Trace each hub cap carefully.
Write down the order of rotation symmetry of each hub cap.

(b) Stick the hub caps into your book.
Mark the centre of rotation symmetry of each hub cap with a cross.

Activity Design a car hub cap which has rotation symmetry.

Before you start, decide what the order of rotation symmetry will be.

Finishing off

Now that you have finished this chapter you should be able to:

- recognise reflection symmetry and draw lines of symmetry
- reflect part of a shape in a line of symmetry to complete it
- recognise rotation symmetry and say what its order is.

Review exercise

1 **(a)** Copy this grid onto squared paper and complete the crossword by answering the questions.

1 Use this to help you find reflection symmetry.

2 This shape has four lines of symmetry.

3 A type of symmetry.

4 Rotation is another type of _____.

5 A line of symmetry is sometimes called an _____ of symmetry.

6 A wheel has this sort of symmetry.

7 From corner to corner of a shape.

8 An axis of symmetry is a straight _____.

9 This shape has rotation symmetry of _____ 3.

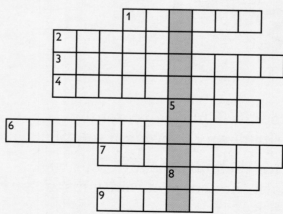

(b) Look at the letters in the shaded squares.
The letters spell the name of a shape.
How many lines of symmetry does the shape have?

2 Which letters of the alphabet have

(a) reflection symmetry (draw the lines on the letters)

(b) rotation symmetry (say what order and mark the centre of rotation)?

Activity

You are going to copy and complete the picture below.

First you need to set up your spreadsheet.

1 Open a new sheet in Excel.
2 Click on the top left corner to select the whole sheet.
3 Select **Format**, **Row**, **Height**, and set to 20.
4 Select **Format**, **Column**, **Width**, and set to 2.57.
5 Click on **Format**, **Cells**, **Border**. Choose the thin line from the **Style** box, then click the **Inside** icon and **OK**.
6 Click on **E** along the top row to select column **E**.
7 Go to **Format**, **Cells**, **Border**. Choose the sort of line you want as the line of symmetry, then click on ⊞ and **OK**.

Now you can copy the picture below.

8 Click on the cell you want to colour.
9 Click on the arrow to the right of the fill icon 🖌 and choose the colour you want.

Now you can complete the picture.

10 Colour more cells to reflect what you have already done in the line of symmetry.
11 Now **Save** or **Print** your picture.

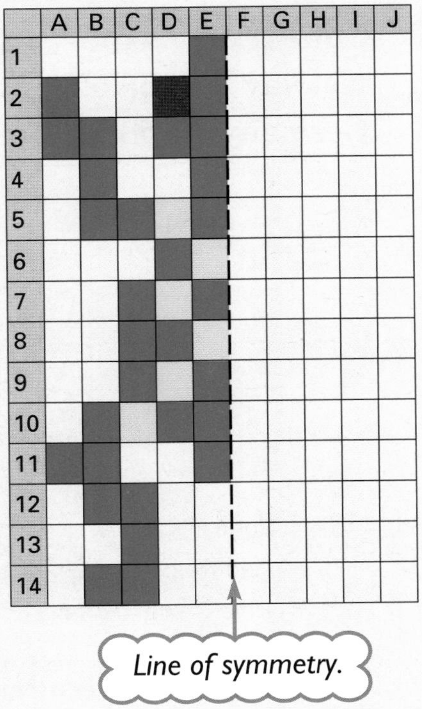

Line of symmetry.

On squared paper, design your own symmetrical drawing.
Use Excel to draw and colour your design.
Print out your design.

In a ski race, Sven takes 58.71 seconds and Karl takes 58.62 seconds.

Alan

Which time is longer? Who is the faster skier?

58.71 is more than 58.62. The 58s are the same but 0.6 is less than 0.7. Karl is the faster skier.

Sophie

Task

Copy and complete the chart for each skier.

Position	Skier	Country	Time	Time from leader
1st	Karl Smit	Norway	58.62	0.00
2nd	Sven Miller	Germany	58.71	0.09
3rd				
4th				
5th				
6th				
7th				
8th				

Results

André Kjus (Austria)	58.86	John Hill (USA)	58.77
Jean Pierre Crux (France)	58.92	Seb Peterson (Switzerland)	58.83
Alain Gross (Croatia)	58.72	Pete Baxter (Britain)	58.90

 Explain what the last column, 'Time from leader', means.

 In a 400 metres race, two athletes are given the same time of 53.48 seconds. Is it a dead heat? Explain your answer.

Exercise

1 Look at the number 58.62 .

(a) What is the 5 worth?
(b) What is the 6 worth?
(c) What is the 2 worth?

2 Look at this number line.
What decimal numbers do the arrows point to?

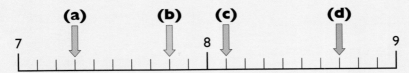

3 Copy this number line.

Put these numbers in the correct place.

7.05, 7.02, 7.14, 7.16, 7.19

4 Put these numbers in order, smallest first (a number line may help).

46.21, 46.2, 45.98, 45.9, 46

5 Enter 10 on a calculator.
Divide it by 2.
The 5 is worth 5 units.

(a) Divide it by 2 again.
What is the 5 worth?

(b) Divide it by 2 again.
What is the 5 worth now?

Scales and dials

Tabby, you are getting too fat!

Mercy

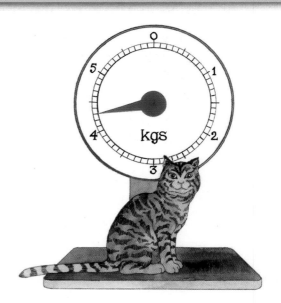

kgs

? **How heavy is Tabby?**
What are the units?

? **What is one small division?**

Task

Draw a 30 cm ruler which shows the different scales on it.

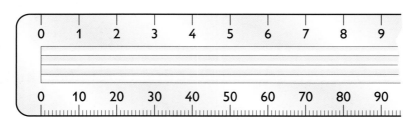

On your drawing explain what the units of each scale are.
Describe how the scales are divided up.

Look at the pictures below.
All these are used for measuring things around the house.

? **What does each one measure?**
What measurements do the pictures show?
Remember to give the units in your answer.

(a)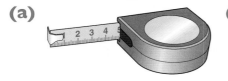

(b)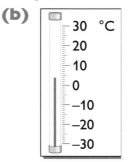

(c)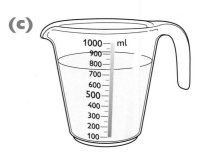

Exercise

1   Look at this thermometer.

   (a) What does it measure?
   (b) What are the units?
   (c) What is one big division?
   (d) What is one small division?
   (e) What is Yuri's temperature?

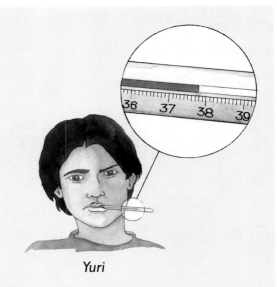

Yuri

2   **(a)** What instruments do you use to measure time?
   (b) What scales do they have?

Activity   Make a poster showing four or more measuring devices.
Draw the scales on each device.
Explain the units of measurement used.

Addition and subtraction of decimals

Roger needs a car park ticket.
Look at his money.

Darlington Station
Parking £2.60
Coins accepted
£2 £1 50p 20p 10p 5p

Exact money only. No change given.

Does he have the correct change?

Task

Play **'Money counts'**, a game for two people.

Aim:

To make a total as near £10 as you can.

Karl

I have a 3 and a 5. I can choose column 3 row 5 or column 5 row 3.

Rules:

1 Take turns to throw two dice.
2 Find the two squares that match your throw.
3 Cover one of these squares with a counter.
4 After three turns, find your total.
5 Use a calculator to check.

⚠ 9p is the same as £0.09.

❓ **Which is nearer to £10: £10.05 or £9.90?**

	1	2	3	4	5	6
6	9p	£4	£0.81	£2.82	£1.30	61p
5	£4.30	£3.46	£3.93	£5.28	£0.79	£3.41
4	96p	£0.56	4p	77p	£3.00	£4.98
3	£0.74	£2.79	32p	£4.05	£1.55	£6.37
2	£3.71	£0.39	£4.50	£2.56	8p	24p
1	£5.30	62p	£1.98	£5.28	£0.78	£6.07

❓ **Look at Alan's shopping list. He used a calculator to add it. What mistake has he made? What should the total be?**

Shopping List
Coke 43p
Lollipop 5p
Sandwich £1.98

49.98

Exercise

Look at the map below.
Find the five places marked with red dots.

	Horncastle	Oxcombe	Mavis Enderby	Claxby Puckacre	Bag Enderby
Horncastle		10.3 km	16.1 km	10.9 km	14.1 km
Oxcombe	10.3 km		16.2 km	18.5 km	8.8 km
Mavis Enderby	16.1 km	16.2 km		8.4 km	9.2 km
Claxby Puckacre	10.9 km	18.5 km	8.4 km		10.6 km
Bag Enderby	14.1 km	8.8 km	9.2 km	10.6 km	

Look at the distance chart above.

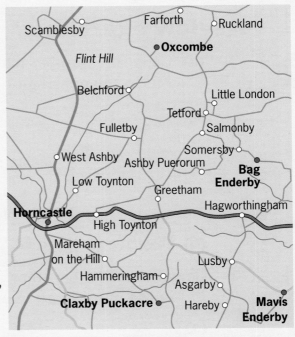

1 **(a)** How far is it from

   (i) Horncastle to
      Bag Enderby

   (ii) Mavis Enderby to
      Oxcombe?

   (b) Which is further,
      (i) or (ii)?

   (c) How much further is it?

2 Which is further, (a) or (b)?

   (a) Horncastle to Oxcombe,
      and then to Mavis
      Enderby.

   (b) Horncastle to Bag Enderby, and then to Claxby Puckacre.

3 Wayne starts at Horncastle.
   He cycles to each of the other villages.
   Then he returns to Horncastle.

   (a) Plan his route.
      How far does he cycle?

   Wayne decides to cycle till he
   reaches 100 km.

   (b) How much further does
      he have
      to cycle?

I want to cycle through all five villages.

Wayne

Finishing off

Review exercise

1 **(a)** Copy this number pattern.
Fill in the missing numbers and words.

	four thousand
400	four hundred
4	four
0.4	four
0.04	four hundredths

(b) Describe the pattern.

2 Copy these number lines.
Fill in the missing numbers.

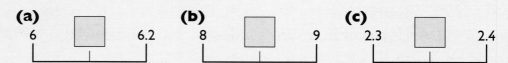

(a) 6 ☐ 6.2   **(b)** 8 ☐ 9   **(c)** 2.3 ☐ 2.4

3 Copy the tables below.
In each row, write a number for B that is bigger than A but smaller than C.
The first line in each table is done for you.

A	B	C
12.0	12.9	13.0
2.1		3.1
6.5		6.9
0.1		1.0

A	B	C
2.4	2.47	2.5
3.6		3.7
21.0		21.1
0.9		1.0

Activity

Play **Place value**, a game for two people.

You need
- place value chart
- 1–9 spinner board
- paper clip and pencil
- six counters each (different colours).

Place value chart

0.001	0.002	0.003	0.004	0.005	0.006	0.007	0.008	0.009
0.01	0.02		0.04	0.05	0.06	0.07	0.08	0.09
0.1	0.2	0.3	0.4	0.5	0.6	0.7	0.8	0.9
1.0	2.0		4.0	5.0	6.0	7.0	8.0	9.0
10.0	20.0	30.0	40.0	50.0		70.0	80.0	90.0
100.0	200.0	300.0	400.0	500.0	600.0	700.0	800.0	900.0

Place value – Biggest number wins

Aim:

To make the biggest number.

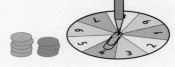

I can't put my counter on 4.0. I have already used that row.

John

Rules:

1 Take turns to spin the paper clip on the spinner board.

2 Put your counter in one of the boxes.
- If you spin a 3, you must put the counter in the '3' **column**.
- You can choose any **row**, but you may only put your counter once in each **row**.
- Both players may put their counter in the same box.

3 After six spins you will each have one counter in every **row**.

4 Add up your total and write it down.

5 The biggest number wins.

Next time, play **Smallest number wins**.

Place value chart

0.001	0.002	0.003	0.004	0.005	0.006	0.007	0.008	0.009
0.01	0.02	0.03	0.04	0.05	0.06	0.07	0.08	0.09
0.1	0.2	0.3	0.4	0.5	0.6	0.7	0.8	0.9
1.0	2.0	3.0	4.0	5.0	6.0	7.0	8.0	9.0
10.0	20.0	30.0	40.0	50.0	60.0	70.0	80.0	90.0
100.0	200.0	300.0	400.0	500.0	600.0	700.0	800.0	900.0

 John is playing **Biggest number wins**.
On his first turn he gets 2. He puts his counter on 200.0.
Why is this a bad choice?

8 Co-ordinates

Megan and Harry are playing **4-in-a-line**.
They take it in turns to place counters on a grid.
The winner is the first person with a line of 4 counters.

Diagonal lines are allowed.

Here is the start of their game.

Harry places a counter at position (3, 2).

*Go 3 squares along from the **start**.*

Then 2 squares up.

Start.

Harry's counter has **co-ordinates** (3, 2).   Harry ● Megan ●

? **Where is Megan's counter?**

Task

Here is a later stage of the game.

1 Write down the co-ordinates of the rest of the counters.

2 Copy Megan and Harry's grid.
Here is the rest of their game.

Megan: (3, 1), (1, 3)

Harry: (2, 0)

Plot Harry and Megan's points on your grid.
Who wins?

3 Play your own game of **4-in-a-line** with a partner.
Write down the co-ordinates of each point you plot.

Harry and Megan have an argument.

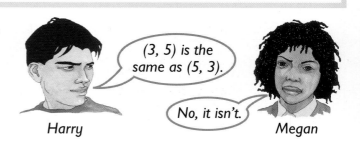

(3, 5) is the same as (5, 3).

No, it isn't.

? **Who is right?**

Harry   Megan

Exercise

Tim draws a map of his town.
The red lines show the roads in his town.

Key
- My house
- School
- Swimming pool
- Cinema
- Shop
- Ice rink
- Park
- Sports centre
- Harry's house
- Michelle's house
- Woods

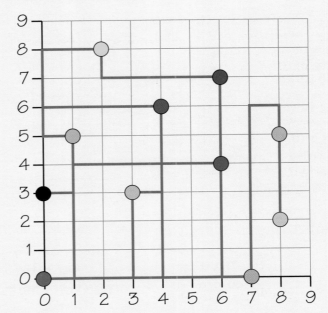

1 What is at these co-ordinates?

(a) $(3, 3)$ **(b)** $(6, 4)$ **(c)** $(4, 6)$

2 Write down the coordinates of these places.

(a) Park **(b)** Shop **(c)** Woods

3 Tim starts at his house and walks to $(1, 0)$ and turns left.
He then walks $(1, 4)$ and turns right.
What is at the end of this road?

4 How does Michelle get from her house to the cinema?

5 Tim and Michelle have an argument.

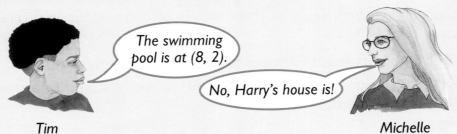

The swimming pool is at (8, 2).

No, Harry's house is!

Tim

Michelle

(a) Who is wrong?
(b) Why does their mistake matter?

Using co-ordinates

Co-ordinates are plotted on **axes**.

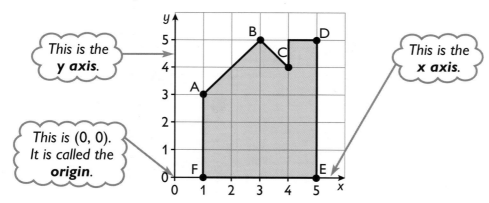

This is the **y axis**.

This is the **x axis**.

This is (0, 0). It is called the **origin**.

The point A has co-ordinates (1, 3).

This is the **x co-ordinate**.

This is the **y co-ordinate**.

? **What are the co-ordinates of points B, C, D, E and F?**

? **Is the point (4, 1) inside the shape?**
What about the point (1, 4)?

Task

For this task you will need some grids like the one above.

1 (a) Plot the points (1, 0), (1, 5), (5, 0) and (5, 5) on a grid and join them up in order.

(b) What have you drawn?

2 (a) Draw a letter on a new grid.

(b) Give the co-ordinates of the corners of your letter to a friend so they can draw it.

3 (a) Make up your own shape and draw it on a new grid.

(b) Give the co-ordinates of the corners of your shape to a friend so they can draw it.

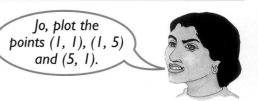

Jo, plot the points (1, 1), (1, 5) and (5, 1).

? **Jo takes a clean sheet of graph paper.**
Then what does she do?

Exercise

1 Write down the co-ordinates of each point plotted below.

(a)

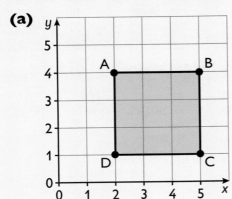

(b)

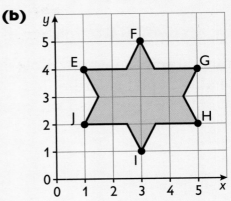

(c)

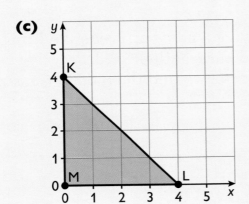

(d)

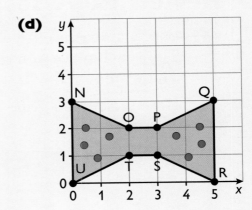

2 Follow these steps.

(a) Draw a pair of axes from 0 to 10.
(b) Plot the following points and join them up.

$(3, 4) \rightarrow (2, 2) \rightarrow (0, 0) \rightarrow (1, 0) \rightarrow (3, 2) \rightarrow$
$(2, 0) \rightarrow (3, 0) \rightarrow (4, 2) \rightarrow (4, 3) \rightarrow (6, 3) \rightarrow$
$(7, 4) \rightarrow (7, 2) \rightarrow (6, 0) \rightarrow (8, 0) \rightarrow (8, 1) \rightarrow$
$(9, 0) \rightarrow (10, 1) \rightarrow (10, 2) \rightarrow (9, 5) \rightarrow (7, 6) \rightarrow$
$(5, 6) \rightarrow (4, 7) \rightarrow (4, 8) \rightarrow (3, 7) \rightarrow (2, 8) \rightarrow$
$(2, 7) \rightarrow (1, 6) \rightarrow (0, 6) \rightarrow (1, 5) \rightarrow (2, 5) \rightarrow$
$(3, 4) \rightarrow (3, 2)$

(c) Now plot these points and join them up.
$(7, 0) \rightarrow (8, 2) \rightarrow (8, 1) \rightarrow (8, 3) \rightarrow (9, 4)$
(d) Now put a dot at $(2, 6)$ and at $(0, 6)$.

What have you drawn?

Finishing off

Now that you have finished this chapter you should:

● understand the words **plot**, **co-ordinates**, **axes** and **origin**
● be able to plot co-ordinates
● be able to write down the co-ordinates of a point.

Review exercise

1 Sophie and Alan are playing a game of **Treasure hunt**.
They each place four gold bars on their grid.
The winner is the first person to find the hidden treasure.

Here is Sophie's grid.

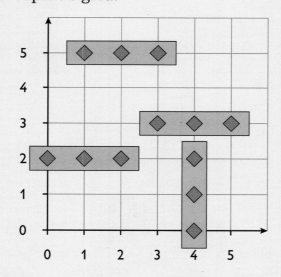

(a) Alan guesses the point (2, 4).
Does Sophie answer 'Yes' or 'No'?

(b) Next turn, Alan guesses the point (4, 3).
What does Sophie answer?

(c) Alan tries a point next to (4, 3).
List the 4 possible points.
For each one say 'Yes' or 'No'.

(d) Write down the co-ordinates of all the points with treasure.

2 Write down the co-ordinates of each point plotted below.

(a)

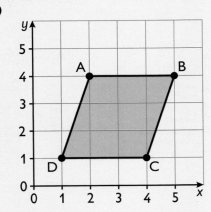

(b)

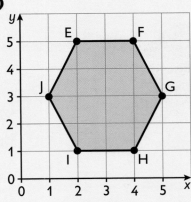

3 Draw a pair of axes from 0 to 6.

(a) Plot the points (1, 2), (4, 2) and (4, 5).

(b) Mark a fourth point to make a square.
What are the co-ordinates of this point?

4 Follow these steps.

(a) Draw a pair of axes from 0 to 12.
(b) Plot the following points and join them up.
    (2, 0) → (1, 3) → (1, 4) → (2, 6) → (4, 7) →
    (8, 7) → (10, 6) → (10, 4) → (8, 5) → (7, 4) →
    (6, 4) → (6, 6) → (7, 7) → (8, 6)
(c) Now plot these points and join them up.
    (2, 6) → (1, 6) → (0, 5)
(d) Now plot these points and join them up.
    (10, 4) → (12, 4) → (10, 3) → (9, 1) → (8, 1) →
    (9, 3) → (8, 4) → (7, 0) → (6, 0) → (6, 3) →
    (3, 4) → (3, 0) → (2, 0)
(e) Now plot these points and join them up.
    (8, 4) → (10, 3)
(f) Now put a dot at (9, 6).

What have you drawn?

Activity Play your own game of **Treasure hunt** with a partner
(see question 1).

SU

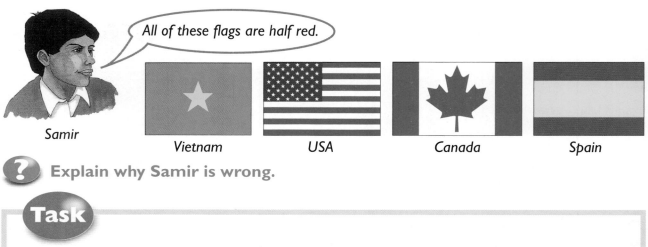

Samir

All of these flags are half red.

Vietnam   USA   Canada   Spain

? **Explain why Samir is wrong.**

Task

1 What fraction is red in these flags?

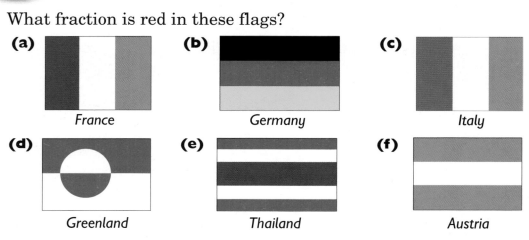

(a) France

(b) Germany

(c) Italy

(d) Greenland

(e) Thailand

(f) Austria

2 What fraction is **(a)** white **(b)** green in these flags?

(i) Ireland

(ii) Nigeria

3 Design a flag which is $\frac{1}{2}$ red, $\frac{1}{4}$ blue and $\frac{1}{4}$ green.

? **Look at these flags.**

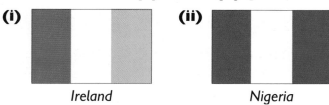

Switzerland

Panama

Romania

Approximately what fraction is red in each flag?

Exercise

1 What fraction of each of these flags is blue?

(a)

(b)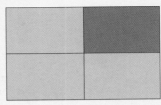

(c)

(d)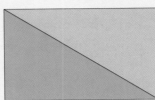

2 Copy these flags and colour them in.

(a) 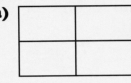 $\frac{1}{2}$ red

$\frac{1}{4}$ yellow

$\frac{1}{4}$ green

(b) 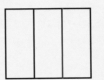 $\frac{2}{3}$ green

$\frac{1}{3}$ red

(c)  $\frac{3}{4}$ blue

$\frac{1}{4}$ red

(d)  $\frac{1}{5}$ blue

$\frac{1}{5}$ yellow

$\frac{3}{5}$ red

3 **(a)** $\frac{1}{2}$ of a flag is blue. The rest is green. What fraction is green?

(b) $\frac{1}{4}$ of a flag is red. The rest is yellow. What fraction is yellow?

(c) $\frac{1}{3}$ of a flag is orange. The rest is green. What fraction is green?

(d) $\frac{3}{5}$ of a flag is white. The rest is red. What fraction is red?

4 Copy and complete these.

(a) $\frac{1}{2} + \boxed{} = 1$ **(b)** $\frac{3}{4} + \boxed{} = 1$ **(c)** $\frac{1}{3} + \boxed{} = 1$ **(d)** $\frac{2}{5} + \frac{1}{5} + \boxed{} = 1$

Activity

1 Copy the flag on the right.

Colour in $\frac{1}{2}$ of the flag. Leave the rest white.

2 Make another copy of the flag on the right.

Colour in $\frac{3}{4}$.

Choose another colour and colour in

the other $\frac{1}{4}$.

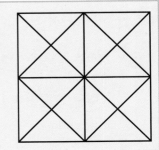

Finding fractions

Wayne and Ali share 12 Smarties equally.

 How many Smarties do they have each?

 *I have $\frac{1}{2}$ of the Smarties.*

Ali

Wayne and Ali eat their Smarties! John now joins them.
They share 12 more Smarties equally between them.

 How many Smarties do they each have this time?
What fraction of the Smarties does John have?
What fraction of the Smarties do Wayne and Ali have between them?

Task

1 Copy and complete these statements.

   (a) $\frac{1}{2}$ of 12 = ☐   **(b)** $\frac{1}{3}$ of 12 = ☐   **(c)** $\frac{2}{3}$ of 12 = ☐

2 (a) Draw 12 circles like the ones below. Use 4 colours to show how 12 Smarties can be shared equally between 4 people.

   (b) A group of people share out the 12 Smarties equally.
   They get 2 each.
   How many people are there?

3 Copy and complete these.

   (a) $\frac{1}{4}$ of 12 = ☐   **(b)** $\frac{3}{4}$ of 12 = ☐   **(c)** $\frac{1}{6}$ of 12 = ☐

4 You share out 20 Smarties equally between a group of people.
   How many people are there in the group?
   There is more than one answer here.

 **How many people can share out 100 Smarties equally?**
What about 1000 Smarties?

Exercise

1 Find $\frac{1}{2}$ of these numbers.

(a) 16   (b) 24   (c) 30   (d) 54   (e) 17

2 Find $\frac{1}{4}$ of these numbers.

(a) 8   (b) 16   (c) 20   (d) 100   (e) 10

3 Now find $\frac{3}{4}$ of the numbers in question 2.

4 Copy these Smarties patterns.

(a) Colour in $\frac{1}{3}$ of the Smarties.

(b) What fraction of the Smarties are uncoloured?

5 What fraction of these Smarties are red?

6 Draw 8 circles like the ones on the right.

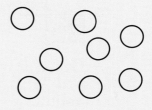

(a) Colour $\frac{1}{2}$ of the Smarties in red.

(b) Colour $\frac{1}{4}$ of the Smarties in blue.

(c) Colour the rest in yellow.

(d) What fraction of the Smarties are yellow?

Activity

1 Jo picks 10 Smarties.
Some are orange, the others are blue.
She puts them in a row. The orange ones are on the left.
Draw all the possible ways, like this one.

Jo

 $\frac{1}{10} = 0.1$ are orange $\frac{9}{10} = 0.9$ are blue

2 Another time, Jo picks 6 Smarties in 3 colours.
Draw all the possibilities now.
Here is one example.

$\frac{1}{6}$ are orange $\frac{2}{6} = \frac{1}{3}$ are blue $\frac{3}{6} = \frac{1}{2}$ are yellow

Equivalent fractions

Meena designs a badge.
She colours 3 out of 6 rectangles in red.

 What fraction is $\frac{3}{6}$ equivalent to?

I can write this as a fraction. $\frac{3}{6}$ of the badge is red.

Meena

Jack colours the badge differently.
He colours 2 out of 6 rectangles in green.

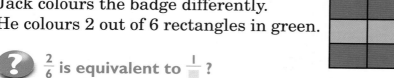

 $\frac{2}{6}$ is equivalent to $\frac{1}{\square}$?

$\frac{4}{6}$ rectangles are blue. What fraction is equivalent?

*This is called **cancelling** the fraction.*

Task

1 Copy and complete the statements for each badge.

(a)

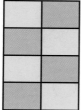

Green $\frac{4}{\square} = \frac{1}{\square}$

Yellow $\frac{\square}{8} = \frac{1}{\square}$

(b)

Blue $\frac{2}{\square} = \frac{1}{\square}$

Red $\frac{6}{\square} = \frac{3}{\square}$

(c)

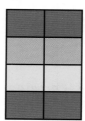

Blue $\frac{\square}{8} = \frac{1}{\square}$

Green $\frac{\square}{8} = \frac{1}{\square}$

Yellow $\frac{\square}{8} = \frac{1}{\square}$

2 Write statements like those in question 1 for these badges.

(a)

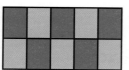

(b)

(c)

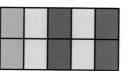

3 Copy and colour in this badge.

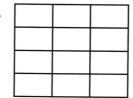

$\frac{1}{2}$ is red

$\frac{1}{4}$ is yellow

$\frac{1}{6}$ is blue

$\frac{1}{12}$ is green

 How many fractions can you find that are equivalent to $\frac{1}{2}$?
What about $\frac{1}{4}$?

Exercise

1 Copy and complete the statements for these badges.

(a)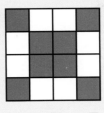

Blue $\dfrac{\blacksquare}{16} = \dfrac{\blacksquare}{\blacksquare}$

White $\dfrac{\blacksquare}{16} = \dfrac{\blacksquare}{\blacksquare}$

(b)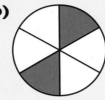

Red $\dfrac{\blacksquare}{6} = \dfrac{1}{\blacksquare}$

White $\dfrac{\blacksquare}{6} = \dfrac{2}{\blacksquare}$

(c)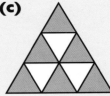

White $\dfrac{\blacksquare}{9} = \dfrac{\blacksquare}{3}$

Purple $\dfrac{\blacksquare}{9} = \dfrac{2}{\blacksquare}$

2 Write statements like those in question 1 for these badges.

(a)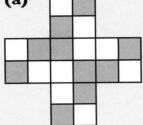

(b)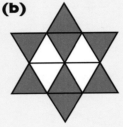

(c)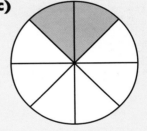

3 Which of these badges are coloured correctly?

(a) $\dfrac{1}{2}$ pink **(b)** $\dfrac{1}{2}$ green **(c)** $\dfrac{1}{4}$ white **(d)** $\dfrac{1}{3}$ white

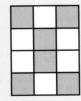 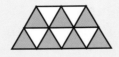

Activity

1 Design a badge that uses 12 squares.
Use 2 colours only.
Write down the fraction of the badge in each colour.

2 Now design another badge with 12 squares.
This time use 3 colours.
Again, write down the fraction of the badge in each colour.

Simple percentages

50% is $\frac{1}{2}$

50% is 50 out of 100

50% is 0.5

50% is $\frac{50}{100}$

50% is 0.50

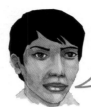 **Which of these statements are true?**

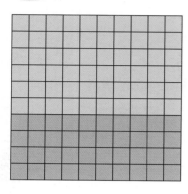

Humza

60 out of 100 squares are blue. $\frac{60}{100}$ are blue. 60% is blue.

40 out of 100 squares are purple. $\frac{40}{100}$ are purple. 40% are purple.

Kim

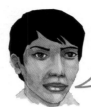 **What fraction is equivalent to $\frac{60}{100}$?**

Task

I Look at the grids below.

   (a) What fraction is in each colour?

   (b) Write down the percentage in each colour.

(i) 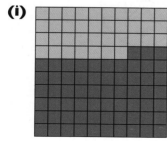 **(ii)** 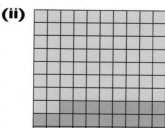 **(iii)**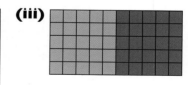

 (iv) 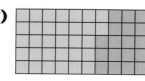 **(v)**  **(vi)**

2 Draw a 10 by 10 grid. Choose 2 colours.

   (a) Shade 25% in one colour.   **(b)** Shade 75% in the other colour.

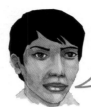 **What needs to be shaded to show $\frac{1}{2}$% on a 10 by 10 grid?**
What about 200%?

Exercise

1 There are 100 insects in the grid.

   (a) What percentage are ladybirds?

   (b) What percentage are butterflies?

   (c) What percentage are bees?

   (d) What do these 3 percentages add up to?

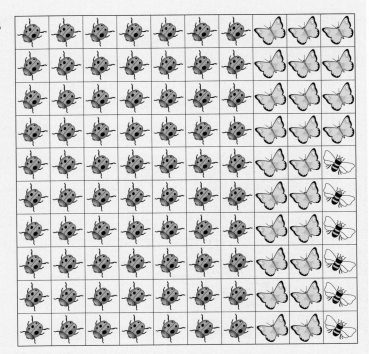

 2 What percentage of each insect is there in the pictures below?

Write the answers as fractions first.

(a)

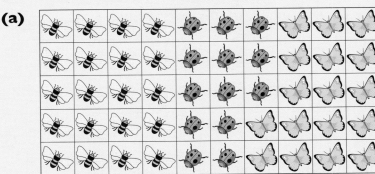

(b)

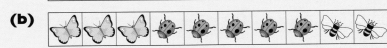

3 There are 10 insects on some flowers.

   10% are bees   40% are butterflies   50% are ladybirds

Draw the insects.

Activity Use a 10 by 10 square. Make a picture or pattern.

Colour   50% in colour 1   20% in colour 2   30% in colour 3

Finishing off

Now that you have finished this chapter you should know:

- the meaning of the terms **half**, **quarter**, **third**, **fifth**, **tenth**, **equivalent fraction**, **percentage**.

Review exercise

1 **(a)** Copy the following flags. Colour in $\frac{1}{2}$ of each flag.

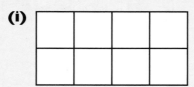

(b) What percentage is coloured?

(c) Copy and complete these statements. Use the flags to help you.

(i) $\frac{\blacksquare}{8} = \frac{1}{2}$ **(ii)** $\frac{5}{\blacksquare} = \frac{1}{2}$

2 **(a)** Copy these flags. Colour in $\frac{1}{3}$ of each flag.

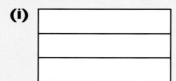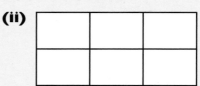

(b) Write an equivalent fraction to $\frac{1}{3}$. Use flag (ii) to help you.

3 **(a)** What fraction of the badges is coloured?

(b) Copy and complete this statement.

$$\frac{1}{5} = \frac{\blacksquare}{10} = \frac{\blacksquare}{100} = \blacksquare\%$$

4 There are 16 Smarties. How many Smarties are red when

(a) $\frac{1}{2}$ are red

(b) $\frac{1}{4}$ are red

(c) $\frac{3}{4}$ are red?

5 Look at the grids below.
   (a) What percentage is coloured?
   (b) What fraction is coloured?
   (c) What percentage is not coloured?

(i) 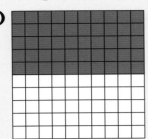   **(ii)** 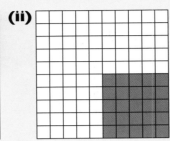   **(iii)**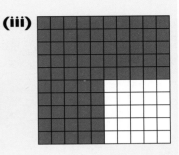

6 Copy the grids below.
Colour in 50% on each grid.

(a) 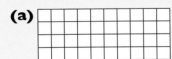   **(b)** 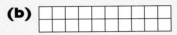   **(c)**

7 Copy the grids below.
Colour in 25% on each grid.

(a)    **(b)**   **(c)**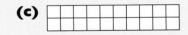

Activity

Look at the questions in this grid.
All the answers are $\frac{1}{4}$, $\frac{1}{2}$, $\frac{3}{4}$ or 1.
Colour the boxes red for $\frac{1}{4}$, blue for $\frac{1}{2}$, yellow for $\frac{3}{4}$ and
green for 1. Find the secret picture.

$7\% + 43\%$	50%	$62\% - 12\%$	$25\% + 25\%$	$100\% - 50\%$	$\frac{50}{100}$	0.5	$\frac{2}{4}$	$2 \times 25\%$
$20\% + 30\%$	$\frac{5}{10}$	$\frac{1}{4}$	$\frac{500}{1000}$	$\frac{24}{48}$	0.500	Half	$\frac{30}{60}$	0.50
$\frac{1}{2}$	0.50	$30\% - 5\%$	$\frac{1}{4} + \frac{1}{4}$	$\frac{1}{2}$ of 1	$\frac{40}{80}$	$2 \times 25\%$	$\frac{1}{2} + \frac{1}{4}$	$5 \times 10\%$
$45\% + 5\%$	$\frac{5}{20}$	0.50	$\frac{25}{100}$	$\frac{44}{88}$	$\frac{3}{6}$	$2 \times \frac{1}{4}$	$3 \times \frac{1}{4}$	$\frac{4}{8}$
$\frac{1}{4}$ of 2	0.25	$16\% + 9\%$	$\frac{3}{4} - \frac{1}{4}$	$17\% + 33\%$	0.50	$1 - \frac{1}{2}$	75%	$68\% - 18\%$
$\frac{7}{14}$	$\frac{6}{12}$	$\frac{1}{2}$ of $\frac{1}{2}$	$1 - \frac{3}{4}$	$\frac{10}{40}$	$\frac{3}{12}$	$1 - \frac{1}{4}$	$\frac{75}{100}$	$\frac{20}{40}$
$\frac{10}{20}$	$75\% - 25\%$	$20\% + 5\%$	25%	$\frac{1}{2} - \frac{1}{4}$	$50\% - 25\%$	$\frac{8}{16}$	$\frac{25}{50}$	$\frac{9}{18}$
$75\% + 25\%$	$\frac{3}{4} + \frac{1}{4}$	$100\% - 75\%$	$\frac{3}{4}$	0.75	$\frac{50}{200}$	$\frac{1}{4}$ of 4	$\frac{7}{7}$	Whole
$2 \times 50\%$	$34\% + 66\%$	$30\% - 5\%$	100%	$\frac{1}{2}$ of 2	$75\% - 50\%$	$0.4 + 0.6$	$\frac{1}{3}$ of 3	$\frac{1}{5} + \frac{4}{5}$
$\frac{1}{3} + \frac{2}{3}$	$\frac{100}{400}$	Quarter	$\frac{3}{10} + \frac{7}{10}$	$\frac{2}{8}$	$\frac{4}{16}$	$50\% + 50\%$	$\frac{2}{5} + \frac{3}{5}$	$\frac{1}{2} + \frac{1}{2}$

10 Types of number

Multiples

Jack makes buns. He sells them in packs of 4.

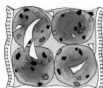 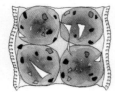 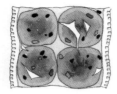

 How many buns are there in 3 packs?
How do you work this out?

> The answer is a **multiple** of 4. It is 3 lots of 4.

Jack

Task

1 Copy and complete the table.

Number of packs	1	2	3	4	5	10
Number of buns	4					

2 What pattern do you notice in the answers?

3 Shade in your answers on a copy of the grid below.

1	2	3	4	5	6	7	8	9	10
11	12	13	14	15	16	17	18	19	20
21	22	23	24	25	26	27	28	29	30
31	32	33	34	35	36	37	38	39	40
41	42	43	44	45	46	47	48	49	50
51	52	53	54	55	56	57	58	59	60
61	62	63	64	65	66	67	68	69	70
71	72	73	74	75	76	77	78	79	80
81	82	83	84	85	86	87	88	89	90
91	92	93	94	95	96	97	98	99	100

4 Shade in the number of buns for 6 packs onwards.
What patterns are there?

Jack now makes bigger packs of buns.

 He makes 30 buns. How many packs does he make?
Next he makes 40 buns.
How many complete packs does he make? How many buns are left over?

Exercise

1

(a) How many arrows are there?
(b) How did you work it out?

2 (a) Write down the first 10 multiples of 2.
(b) Write down the first 10 multiples of 3.
(c) Underline any multiples that are the same for 2 and 3.

These are called **common multiples**.

SU

3 Copy and complete the puzzles. In the first puzzle $5 \times 3 = 15$ has been done for you.

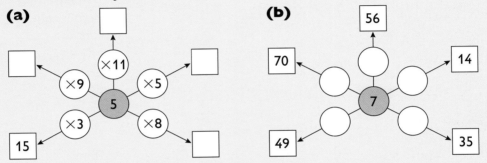

4 Which of these numbers are **not** multiples of 8?

8, 14, 24, 30, 40, 56, 77, 80, 88, 100, 108

Activity

SU

1 Shade in the multiples of 4 on a copy of the 'spiral' grid below. What patterns do you notice?

73	74	75	76	77	78	79	80	81	82
72	43	44	45	46	47	48	49	50	83
71	42	21	22	23	24	25	26	51	84
70	41	20	7	8	9	10	27	52	85
69	40	19	6	1	2	11	28	53	86
68	39	18	5	4	3	12	29	54	87
67	38	17	16	15	14	13	30	55	88
66	37	36	35	34	33	32	31	56	89
65	64	63	62	61	60	59	58	57	90
100	99	98	97	96	95	94	93	92	91

2 Try some different multiples. Use another copy of the grid.

Square numbers

Kim is making squares. She numbers them in a spiral pattern.

1

1	2
4	3

7	8	9
6	1	2
5	4	3

7	8	9	10
6	1	2	11
5	4	3	

? **How do you complete the fourth square?**

I am numbering clockwise.

Kim

Task

1 Continue to make Kim's squares bigger. You need only one diagram. Use different colours.

2 Copy and fill in this table of results.

Length of the side	1	2	3	4	5	6	7	8	9	10
New colour	Yellow	Orange	Red	Brown						
Number of new small squares	1	3	5							
Total number of small squares	1	4	9							

These are the square numbers.

? **What patterns do you notice in your table?**

? **How many small squares are used when the length of the side is 11? How can you find the 20th square number?**

Exercise

1 Samir colours his square pattern differently.

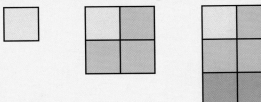
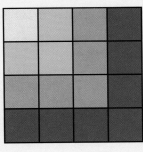

Copy and complete this table.

Length of the side	1	2	3	4	5	6
New colour	Pink	Green	Blue	Purple		
Number of new small squares	1					
Total number of small squares	1					

2 **(a)** Samir draws a square of length 7.
   How many small squares does it have?
   (b) How do you work this out?
   (c) Samir makes a big square with 64 small squares.
   How long is each side of this square?

3 Continue this sequence up to 10 squared.

   1 squared = 1 × 1 = 1
   2 squared = 2 × 2 = 4
   3 squared = 3 × 3 =
   4 squared =   =

4 A quick way to write 3 squared is 3^2.
   Work out the answers to these.

   (a) 6^2 **(b)** 10^2 **(c)** 11^2 **(d)** 20^2 **(e)** 50^2

Activity Use the x^2 button on a calculator to find all the square numbers up to 20^2.

Factors

This is a factor spider for the number 12.

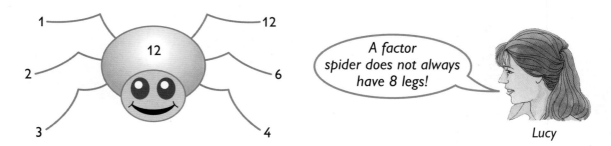

Lucy

A factor spider does not always have 8 legs!

These numbers are factors of 12. They divide exactly into 12.

$1 \times 12 = 12$ $2 \times 6 = 12$ and $3 \times 4 = 12$

? **How many factors do you think the number 24 has?**

Task

1 (a) Copy and complete the following for the number 24.

$1 \times \boxed{} = 24$ $2 \times \boxed{} = 24$ $3 \times \boxed{} = 24$ $4 \times \boxed{} = 24$

(b) Draw a factor spider for the number 24.

2 (a) Draw the factor spider for the number 16.
(b) Why is this special?

3 (a) Draw the factor spider for the number 17.
(b) Can you think of another factor spider that has only 2 legs?

36 pencils are shared among a group of people.

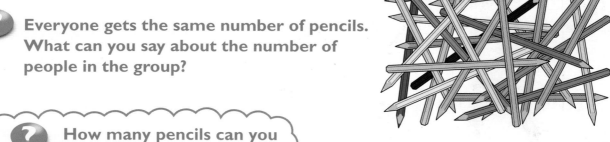

? **Everyone gets the same number of pencils. What can you say about the number of people in the group?**

? **How many pencils can you see in this picture?**

Exercise

1 **(a)** Copy and complete the following multiplication sums.

    (i) ☐ × 10 = 10

    (ii) 2 × ☐ = 10

 (b) What are the factors of 10?

2 **(a)** Copy and complete the following to find the factors of 20.

    (i) 1 × ☐ = 20

    (ii) ☐ × 10 = 20

    (iii) ☐ × ☐ = 20

 (b) How many factors does the number 20 have?

3 **(a)** Write out all the multiplication sums for the number 30.

 (b) Draw the factor spider for the number 30.

4 Match the numbers to the factor spiders.   45   20   18

5 £28 is shared out equally between some children. How many children can there be?

6 How many children can share out £100 equally?

> Questions 5 and 6 have more than one answer. How many can you find?

Activity

1 Draw the factor spider for 100.

2 Draw the factor spider for 1000.

3 Choose a number of your own.
Draw its factor spider.
You may want to use a calculator to help you find the factors.

Prime numbers

5 squares can be put together to make 2 rectangles.

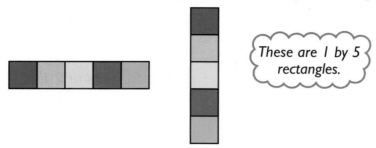

These are 1 by 5 rectangles.

5 is a **prime number**. It has exactly 2 factors.

The factors of 5 are 1 and 5.

6 squares can be put together to make 4 rectangles.

6 is **not** a prime number because it has more than 2 factors.

 What are the factors of 6?

Task

1 (a) Draw all the different rectangles you can make with 7 squares.
(b) Is 7 a prime number?

2 (a) Draw all the rectangles you can make with 8 squares.
(b) Is 8 a prime number?

3 Take other numbers between 2 and 20.
Find out if these numbers are prime.

 1 is not a prime number.

Christina

All prime numbers are odd.

You are wrong Christina.

Alan

 Why is Christina wrong?

Exercise

1 Here are three of the rectangles you can make with 24 squares.

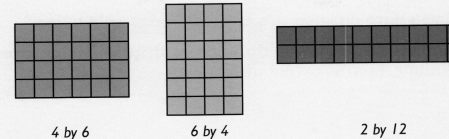

4 by 6   6 by 4   2 by 12

(a) There are 5 more rectangles. What are they?

(b) Is 24 a prime number?

2 Write down all the numbers between 20 and 30.
Circle the prime numbers.

3

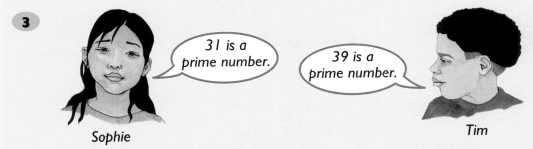

31 is a prime number.

39 is a prime number.

Sophie   Tim

One of them is wrong. Who is it, Sophie or Tim? Why?

4 Which of these numbers are prime?

| 32 | 43 | 55 | 61 | 100 |

5 These numbers are **not** prime. How can you tell?

(a) 4, 14, 20, 56, 84 and 100

(b) 5, 10, 20, 25, 40, 65 and 100

(c) 22, 33, 55, 77 and 99

Activity   13 P in a R L T stands for 13 Players in a Rugby League Team.
Try these other word puzzles. All the numbers are prime numbers.

1 11 P in a F T   **2** 7 D in a W   **3** 101 D

4 S W and the 7 D   **5** 3 B M   **6** 7 P in a N T

7 31 D in J   **8** 3 F in a Y   **9** 13 H in a P of C

Finishing off

Now that you have finished this chapter you should know:

- the meaning of the terms **odd number**, **multiple**, **square number**, **even number**, **factor**, **prime number**.

Review exercise

1 Look at these numbers.

(a) Write down the odd numbers.

(b) Which numbers are multiples of 4?

(c) Write down the square numbers.

(d) Find two factors of 16.

(e) Which numbers are a multiple of both 3 and 4?

(f) Which number is a factor of both 22 and 33?

(g) Which two numbers multiply to make 56?

(h) Find three numbers that add up to 32.

2 **(a)** Use the digits 4 and 6 to make a square number.

(b) Use the digits 3 and 5 to make a prime number.

(c) Use the digits 3 and 6 to make a multiple of 4.

3 One of these numbers is **not** a multiple of 5.
Which number is the odd one out?

5   25   60

56   100

4 Find the sets of numbers in the number search.
Each set is hidden in a straight line. It might run across, up or down, or diagonally.

(a) The first 7 even numbers.
(b) The first 9 square numbers.
(c) The first 5 prime numbers.
(d) The factors of 32 (in order).
(e) The first 5 multiples of 4.
(f) The multiples of 9 from 4×9.

(g) The doubling sequence from 2 (6 numbers).

6	2	1	11	12	41	15	3
1	2	4	8	16	32	4	2
7	3	9	6	20	5	3	10
9	14	16	7	8	5	20	22
21	23	25	9	7	10	16	20
34	35	36	11	12	11	12	3
8	3	49	3	5	17	8	14
15	15	64	32	16	8	4	2
99	90	81	72	63	54	45	36

5 The number in the square is made from multiplying the numbers in the two circles at either side.
Copy and complete the triangle puzzles.

(a)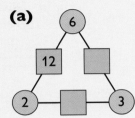

(b)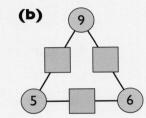

(c)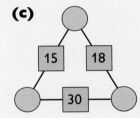

Investigation

Look how these triangles are made.

1 Copy the diagrams and count the number of dots.
Write the answers underneath the diagrams.

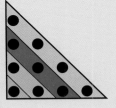

The number of dots are the **triangular numbers**.

Megan

2 Draw the next 2 diagrams.
Write down the number of dots in each.

3 How do the answers increase?

Length

Look at this ruler.

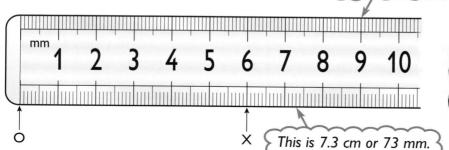

This is 9 cm or 90 mm.

This is 7.3 cm or 73 mm.

Meena

So **7.3** means **7** whole centimetres and **3** millimetres.

? How do you write the length OX?

? Copy and complete these conversions.

300 cm = ◻ metres   2000 mm = ◻ m

6 metres = ◻ cm   4 metres = ◻ mm

Remember!
100 cm = 1 metre
1000 mm = 1 metre

Task

You will need a ruler, a metre stick and a tape measure.
Measure these objects in centimetres.
Copy the table below and use it to record your results.

Object	Length in cm	Length in given unit	
This book	27.0	27 cm	0 mm
Around your head			mm
Your height		m	cm
Length of your thumbnail			mm
Length of your arm		cm	mm
Length of your pen		cm	mm
Height of the classroom		m	cm
Height of the door		m	cm

? Copy and complete these conversions

4000 m = ◻ km   7 km = ◻ m

Remember!
1000 m = 1 kilometre.

? What other units are used for measuring length?

Exercise

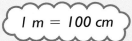

1 cm = 10 mm

1 Change these measurements to millimetres.
   (a) 2 cm   **(b)** 8 cm   **(c)** 10 cm   **(d)** 25 cm   **(e)** $\frac{1}{2}$ cm

2 Change these measurements to centimetres.
   (a) 40 mm   **(b)** 60 mm   **(c)** 150 mm   **(d)** 300 mm   **(e)** 15 mm

3 Change these measurements to metres.
   (a) 200 cm   **(b)** 800 cm   **(c)** 1400 cm
   (d) 2900 cm   **(e)** 50 cm

   1 m = 100 cm

4 Change these measurements to centimetres.
   (a) 5 m   **(b)** 9 m   **(c)** 16 m   **(d)** 99 m   **(e)** $1\frac{1}{2}$ m

5

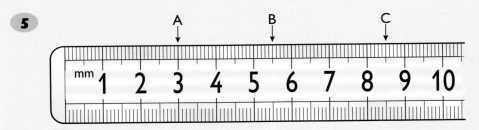

   (a) What is the distance from A to B in **mm**?
   (b) What is the distance from B to C in **cm**?
   (c) What is the distance from A to C in **cm**?

6 Write down the smaller measurement in each of these pairs.
   (a) 17 mm   3.2 cm   **(b)** $2\frac{1}{2}$ cm   24 mm
   (c) 3 m   200 cm   **(d)** $\frac{1}{2}$ m   48 cm
   (e) 4000 m   6 km   **(f)** $1\frac{1}{2}$ km   1200 m

7 Copy and complete this conversion diagram.

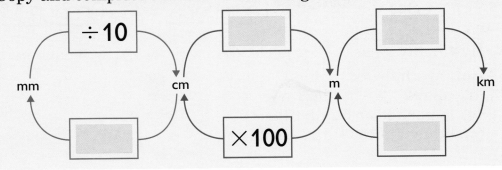

Activity   Do people who have large feet also have large hands?
   Measure your friends' hands and feet to find out.

Capacity (or volume)

Karl is making fizzy orange.

? **What does ml stand for?**

? **How much fizzy orange does Karl make?**
How many litres is this?

Karl makes 2 litres of fizzy orange.

? **How many ml of orange juice does he use?**
How much lemonade does he use?

Fizzy orange

750 ml orange juice
250 ml lemonade

Task

You are planning a party.

1 Decide how many people to invite.

You are going to serve fizzy orange and cola.

200 ml

The capacity
or volume of each glass
is 200 ml.

Karl

Cola   Lemonade   Orange juice

2 How many glasses of **(a)** cola **(b)** fizzy orange will each person drink?
3 How much drink should you buy?
  (a) cola (2 litre bottles)
  (b) lemonade (1 litre bottles)
  (c) orange juice (1 litre cartons)

? **How many centilitres are there in a litre?**

? **What other units are used for capacity?**

Exercise

1 Copy the list of items. Match each item to its capacity.

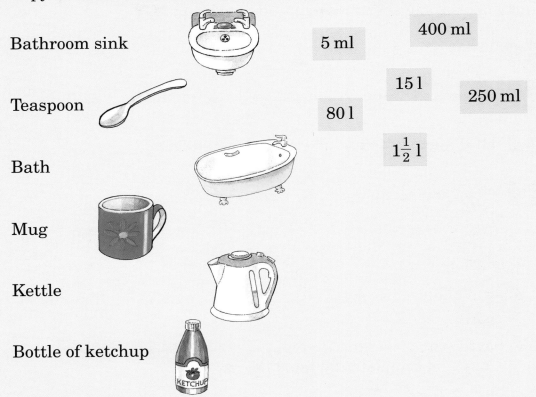

Bathroom sink

Teaspoon

Bath

Mug

Kettle

Bottle of ketchup

5 ml

400 ml

15 l

80 l

250 ml

$1\frac{1}{2}$ l

2 How much liquid is in each of these containers?

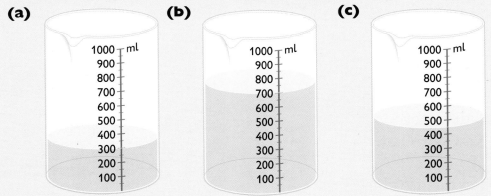

(a) **(b)** **(c)**

3 We should drink 2 litres of water every day.
How much water should we drink in a week? In a year?

4 Melissa buys a 1 litre bottle of shampoo. She uses 25 ml each wash.
How many times can she wash her hair with each bottle?

5 Each person uses about 150 litres of water every day.
How much water is used in your house every day?

Activity Collect some drinks labels that use ml, cl and litres.
Arrange them in order of capacity.

Weight (mass)

Karl makes some shortbread biscuits for his party.

? **What does g mean?**

? **What is the total weight of all the ingredients?**

? **How much does one shortbread biscuit weigh?**

Shortbread

Makes 10 biscuits

150g flour
100g butter
25g white sugar
25g brown sugar

? **Copy and complete these conversions.**

5 kg   =   ☐ g   3000 mg = ☐ g

8000 g = ☐ kg   7 g   = ☐ mg

> Remember!
> 1000 g = 1 kg
> 1000 mg = 1 g

Task

1 Match the object to its weight.
Copy and complete the table below.

2 kg   1 kg   400 g

15 g   100 g   4 kg

Object	Weight
Empty mug	
Iron	
Bag of sugar	
Pen	
Calculator	
New born baby	

2 Find 5 more objects.
Weigh each one and add them to your table.

3 Make a poster showing each object and its weight, from the lightest to the heaviest.

? **What is the weight of (a) a car (b) an elephant?**

? **What other units of weight are there?**

Exercise

su

1 Copy the table below. Put these objects in the correct column.

Tin of beans   *Mobile phone*   *Vacuum cleaner*

Doll   *Textbook*   *Apple*   *Dog*

Computer   *Pencil*   *Desk*

Less than 1000 g (1 kg)	More than 1000 g (1 kg)

2 Ali has one of each of these weights.

1 kg 1000 g   500 g   200 g   100 g   50 g   20 g

Use these weights to make these amounts.

(a) 600 g   **(b)** 150 g   **(c)** 350 g

(d) 1300 g   **(e)** 1 kg 650 g   **(f)** 820 g

(g) $1\frac{1}{2}$ kg

To make 700 g I would use 500 g + 200 g.

Ali

3 An average cat needs 90 g of cat food each day.
Kate has 2 cats.
How many days will a 2 kg bag of cat food last for?

4 A bag of 6 apples weighs 900 g.

(a) How much does 1 apple weigh?

(b) How many apples weigh $1\frac{1}{2}$ kg?

Activity Find out about the cost of sending things in the post.
Make a poster showing how much it would cost to send different things in the post.

Time

Mark and Melissa go to different schools.

Mark

> My school
> starts at five past nine.
> In numbers that is
> 9:05.

Melissa

> My school
> starts at ten minutes
> to 9.

? **How is ten minutes to nine written using numbers?**

? **How do you show that a time is in the morning or afternoon in the 12-hour clock?**

Task

Write your timetable for today at school using the table below.
Mark's day would start like this.

> At school I
> go to registration first.
> It is 5 minutes
> long.

Lesson	Time in words	Time in numbers	Clock	How long for
Registration	Five minutes past nine	9:05 am		5 minutes

? **How do you write 2 o'clock in the afternoon in the 24-hour clock? How did you work it out?**

? **Mark goes to bed at 1935 hours. What is this time on the 12-hour clock?**

? **What other units of time are there?**

Exercise

su

1 Draw these times on an ordinary 12-hour clock face.
- **(a)** 7:15
- **(b)** 11:05
- **(c)** 1:35
- **(d)** 2055
- **(e)** 0440
- **(f)** 1350

2 Write these times in words and then in numbers.

(a) **(b)** **(c)** **(d)** **(e)**

3 **(a)** How many weeks are there in a year?
   (b) How many days are there in a year?
   (c) How many days are there in a leap year?

4 Make a list of the months of the year in order.
   Give the number of days in each month.
   Here is the start of the list.

   January   31 days

5 Look at this calendar.

May 2013

M	T	W	T	F	S	S
		1	2	3	4	5
6	7	8	9	10	11	12
13	14	15	16	17	18	19
20	21	22	23	24	25	26
27	28	29	30	31		

The 10th of May is a Friday.

(a) What day of the week is May 17th?
(b) How many Wednesdays are there in May 2013?
(c) How many weekends are there in May?
(d) What day of the week is May 1st?
(e) What day of the week is the last day of April?
(f) The 1st Monday in May is a holiday.
   What date is it?

6 Work out these.
- **(a)** $\frac{1}{2}$ hour + $\frac{1}{2}$ hour
- **(b)** $\frac{1}{2}$ hour + $\frac{1}{4}$ hour
- **(c)** $1\frac{1}{2}$ hours + $\frac{1}{2}$ hour
- **(d)** $\frac{1}{4}$ hour + $\frac{3}{4}$ hour
- **(e)** $\frac{3}{4}$ hour + $\frac{1}{2}$ hour
- **(f)** $\frac{3}{4}$ hour + $\frac{3}{4}$ hour

Finishing off

Now that you have finished this chapter you should be able to:

- use metric units of length
- use metric units of weight (mass)
- use both the 12-hour and 24-hour clocks.

Review exercise

1 Sort these **metric** units into length, weight (mass) or capacity.

| metre | millilitre | gram | centimetre |

| kilogram | kilometre | litre | millimetre |

Do the same with these **imperial** measures.

| mile | ounce | gallon | stone | yard | pint |

2

Fruity Bread

650 g .... flour
35 g .... butter
100 ml ....milk
10 g .... yeast
150 g .... raisins
250 ml .... water
20 g ....sugar

Fruity Bread

(a) Which ingredients are measured by weight?
(b) Which ingredients are measured by capacity?

3 What amounts do these scales show?
Remember to give the units in your answer.

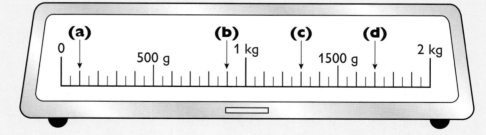

4 What **unit** would be used to measure these?

(a) Your height
(b) Distance to America
(c) How long until your birthday
(d) Length of a mouse
(e) Weight of a bus
(f) How long you can hold your breath

5 Write these times in (i) words and (ii) numbers.

(a) (b)  (c) (d) (e)

6 Write these times in numbers. Use the 24-hour clock.

(a) Half past 7 at night
(b) 20 minutes past 11 in the morning
(c) 5 minutes to 9 at night
(d) 5 minutes past 2 in the afternoon
(e) 25 minutes to 6 in the morning

7 Here is part of a bus timetable.

Tipton	1005
Ottery	1020
Honiton	1055
Feniton	1115

I get on the bus at Ottery and get off at Honiton.

Harry

I get on at Ottery and get off at Feniton.

My journey takes 20 minutes.

Michelle

John

(a) How long is Harry's journey?
(b) Where does Michelle get on and off the bus?
(c) How long is John's journey?

Activity Make a table showing the different units for length, weight (mass) and capacity.
Stick it in the back of your exercise book.

12 Flat shapes

Types of triangle

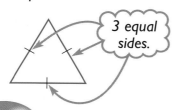

Equilateral — 3 equal sides.

Isosceles — 2 equal sides.

Scalene — All sides different.

Task

1 Use a ruler to measure the sides of these triangles. Copy and complete the table below.

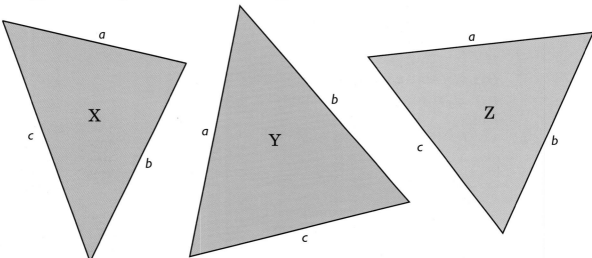

Triangle	Side lengths			Type
	a	**b**	**c**	
X	5 cm			
Y				
Z				

2 Use a protractor to measure the angles in the equilateral triangle. What do you notice?

3 Measure the angles in the isosceles triangle. What do you notice?

The two equal angles in an isosceles triangle are called **base angles**.

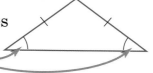

 How do you use a protractor to draw an isosceles triangle?

Exercise

SU

1 Look at each triangle.

    (a) Guess its type by looking at it.

    (b) Check by measuring the sides.

    (c) Write your results in a table like the one in the task.

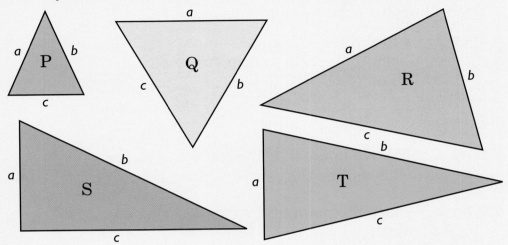

2 Use a protractor to draw an isosceles triangle with base angles of 70°.
Check that two sides are equal.

3 Which of these triangles are

    (a) equilateral

    (b) scalene

    (c) isosceles?

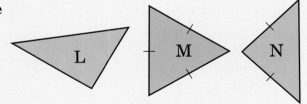

4 Look at this pattern.
There are 25 triangles and 3 squares.

    (a) How many triangles are isosceles?

    (b) How many triangles are equilateral?

    (c) How many triangles are scalene?

Check that you have found all 25 triangles.

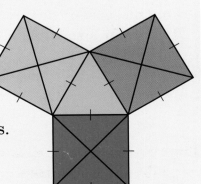

Circles

 Do the right thing!

Follow these steps to draw a perfect circle.
You will need a pair of compasses and a ruler.

Step 1   Place the point of the compasses at the
beginning of the centimetre scale.
Open the pencil to 6 cm.

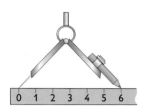

*This is the **radius** of the circle.*

Step 2   Mark a cross on a clean sheet of paper.
This will be the centre of the circle. *Centre.*

Step 3   Place the point of the compasses
on the cross.
Draw the pencil round
to make the circle.

*This is the **circumference**.*

?   **What size is the largest circle you can draw with your compasses?**
What size is the smallest circle you can draw with your compasses?

Task

Look at this picture of a radar screen.
All the circles have the same centre.

Concentric *circles.*

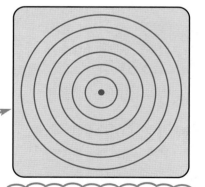

On the screen the circles are 1 cm apart.
The inner circle has a radius of 1 cm.

Draw a full size picture of the radar screen.

This diagram is not full size.

?   **A circle has a radius of 7 cm.**
What is its diameter?
What can you say about the radius and the diameter?
Calculate the diameters of the circles in the task.

*This line is a **diameter** of the circle.*

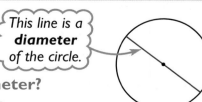

Exercise

1 Use a pair of compasses to draw these circles.

(a) A circle with radius 5 cm.
(b) A circle with radius 7 cm.
(c) A circle with radius 8.4 cm.
(d) A circle with **diameter** 14 cm.

2 (i) Measure the radius of each circle below.
(ii) Work out the diameter of each circle.

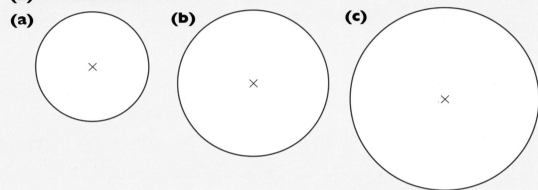

(a) (b) (c)

Activity Follow these steps to draw a **regular hexagon**.

1 Draw a large circle.

2 Do not adjust the compasses.

Use the compasses to make marks around the circumference.
- Draw the first mark anywhere, to start.
- Put the point of the compasses on the first mark to draw the second mark.
- Continue round the circumference.

3 Join the marks with straight lines as shown.

? **How many sides does a hexagon have?**

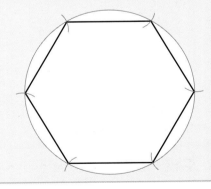

Measure the length of each side of the hexagon.
Measure each angle in the hexagon.

? **Why is it called a regular hexagon?**

Activity Use a pair of compasses to draw a worm.

1 Draw a wavy line.

2 Mark centres along the line.

3 Draw a circle round each centre.

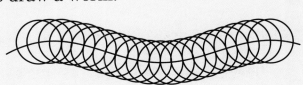

Quadrilaterals

Jack has drawn this plan of a football pitch.
The pitch is a **quadrilateral**.
Most of the shapes are quadrilaterals.

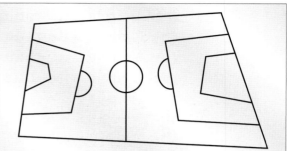

? **What is a quadrilateral?**

? **What is wrong with this football pitch?**

Task

You will need centimetre squared paper, a ruler and a pair of compasses.
You are going to draw a football pitch which is **right**.

Start by copying the diagram below. It is 24 cm long and 16 cm wide.

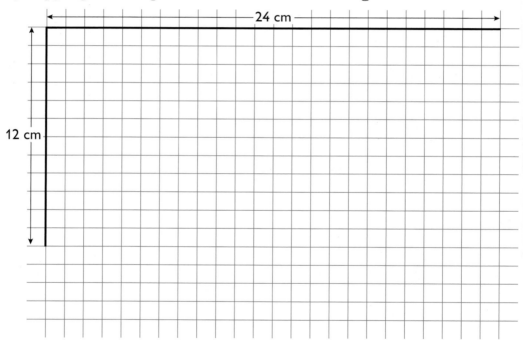

Add all the other markings.
Use a pair of compasses for the circular parts.

? **What have you done to make your pitch right?**

? **Does your pitch have any lines of symmetry?**

? **There should be lots of rectangles on your pitch.
Are any of them squares?**

Exercise

1 **(a)** Use squared paper to draw a rectangle 8 cm long and 4 cm wide.

(b) Cut out the rectangle and fold it to make two squares.
Shade each square in different colours.

2 **(a)** Draw a rectangle which is 10 cm long and 6 cm wide.

(b) Cut out your rectangle.
Can you fold it to make two squares?
Explain your answer.

3 **(a)** Draw a square with sides 7 cm.
Draw a diagonal across the square.

(b) You have made two triangles.
Are they equilateral, isosceles or scalene?
Explain your answer.

4 **(a)** Draw a rectangle 9 cm long and 5 cm wide.
Draw a diagonal across the rectangle.

(b) What sort of triangles have you made?

Activity

You can draw a rectangle without squared paper.
You use a ruler and a **set square**.

1 Draw a line on some plain paper.

2 Put two marks, 8 cm apart.

3 Use the set square to draw two right angles to
the line at your marks.

4 Put a mark 5 cm along each line.

5 Join the two marks to complete the rectangle.

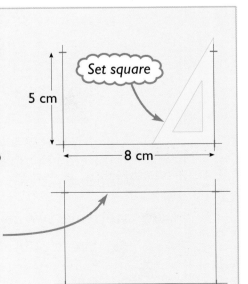

Draw two more rectangles and two squares.
Choose your own length and width.

Finishing off

Now that you have finished this chapter you know:

- that there are three different types of triangle, **equilateral**, **isosceles** and **scalene**
- how to draw circles
- the meanings of **radius** and **diameter**
- that a quadrilateral has four sides
- how to draw squares and rectangles.

Review exercise

1 **(i)** Measure the sides of each triangle.
(ii) Write down the type of each triangle.

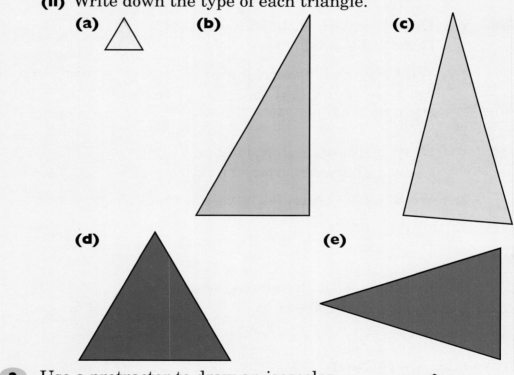

(a) **(b)** **(c)**

(d) **(e)**

2 Use a protractor to draw an isosceles triangle with base angles of 30°. Check that two sides are equal.

3 Here are two concentric circles.

(a) Use a pair of compasses to draw two concentric circles like these.

(b) What is the distance between your circles?

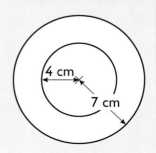

4 **(a)** Use squared paper to draw a rectangle which can be folded into 2 squares.

(b) Cut out your rectangle and test it.

5 **(a)** Use squared paper to draw a rectangle which can be cut into 3 squares.

(b) Cut out your rectangle and test it.

Activity

1 Draw and cut out a square.

2 Draw the two diagonals and cut along the lines.

3 You have cut the square into four triangles. What sort of triangles are they?

4 Place the four triangles on top of each other.
   (a) What do you find?
   (b) What fraction of the square is one triangle?

5 Use two of the triangles to make another square.

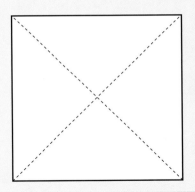

Investigation

1 Draw a rectangle and cut it out.

2 Fold it into four equal parts like this.

? What four shapes have you made?

3 Draw a square and cut it out.

4 Fold it into four equal parts like this.

? What four shapes have you made?

5 Repeat this with different squares and rectangles.

? What do you find?

Multiplying decimals

Christina has a model railway.
She is buying a new train.

Engine

£51.50   25.6 cm

I will have an engine and 6 trucks.

Christina

Truck

£7.25   8.1 cm

Christina writes:

7.25	43.50
× 6	+ 51.50
43.50	95.00

It costs £95.

? **Explain Christina's working.**

? **How long is Christina's new train?**

Task

Here are some more models.

Coach   £16.50   30.5 cm

Flat truck   £8.40   13.3 cm

Small engine   £42.10   10.2 cm

You have £120 to spend on a train.
1 Decide on your train.
2 How much money is left over?
3 How long is your train?

? **How do you do these multiplications?**
   (a) 2.1 × 3   **(b)** 3.21 × 4   **(c)** 12.43 × 5

? **What is 0.125 × 8?**

Exercise

1 Work out these.

   (a) (i) 10×6 **(ii)** 1×6 **(ii)** 0.1×6 **(iv)** 0.01×6 **(v)** 0.001×6

   (b) (i) 30×4 **(ii)** 3×4 **(ii)** 0.3×4 **(iv)** 0.03×4 **(v)** 0.003×4

   (c) (i) 20×7 **(ii)** 2×7 **(ii)** 0.2×7 **(iv)** 0.02×7 **(v)** 0.002×7

What do you notice about the numbers of decimal places in the questions and the answers?

2 Work out these.

   (a) 3.4×2 **(b)** 13.3×3

   (c) 12.2×4 **(d)** 10.1×5

   (e) 6.3×2 **(f)** 7.2×5

   (g) 16.3×3 **(h)** 20.9×5

   (i) 5.12×2 **(j)** 6.05×4

   (k) 1.17×3 **(l)** 1.81×9

3 Work out these.

   (a) 4.1×3 **(b)** 5.2×2

   (c) 6.3×3 **(d)** 10.8×4

   (e) 2.8×2 **(f)** 4.1×5

   (g) 0.03×3 **(h)** 3.125×3

   (i) 1.175×4 **(j)** 1.125×6

4 Find the cost of these.

   (a) 2 painting sets at £6.50 each.

   (b) 3 birthday cards at £1.75 each.

   (c) 6 notepads at £0.25 each.

Dividing decimals

Meena and three friends go to Dragon City takeaway.
They decide to have the meal for 4.

We'll share the cost equally.

Humza

How much will that be each?

Meena

Dragon City
Takeaway

Meal for 2	£14.90
Meal for 3	£21.60
Meal for 4	£29.20
Meal for 6	£37.80

Humza writes:

```
        7.30
    4)29.20
      28
       1 2
       1 2
         00
         00
    £7.30 each
```

Meena writes:

```
    4|29.¹20
       7.30
    £7.30 each
```

? **Explain their working.**
 Which way do you like better?

Task

Look at this menu.

1 Choose 5 items for a meal for 5 friends.

2 They share the cost equally.
 What is the cost per person?

? **How can you check your working?**

Menu

Fried chicken and mushrooms	£3.80
King prawn with tomato	£4.80
Roast duck with pineapple	£5.30
Sweet and sour chicken	£3.80
Beef with peppers	£4.30
Chow mein	£4.20
Prawn fried rice	£4.10
Mixed vegetables	£3.50
Special Foo Yung	£4.00
Egg fried rice	£1.60

? **How do you do these divisions?**
 (a) $2.4 \div 3$?   **(b)** $1.421 \div 7$ **(c)** $124.84 \div 4$

? **What is $12 \div 5$ as a decimal?**

Exercise

1 Work out these.

    (a) $6.8 \div 2$ **(b)** $2.4 \div 3$ **(c)** $5.7 \div 3$

    (d) $0.96 \div 3$ **(e)** $12.5 \div 5$ **(f)** $6.4 \div 4$

    (g) $27.9 \div 9$ **(h)** $14.5 \div 5$ **(i)** $63.8 \div 2$

    (j) $1.05 \div 5$ **(k)** $0.096 \div 6$ **(l)** $0.712 \div 4$

2 Work out these.

    (a) $62.0 \div 2$ **(b)** $49.0 \div 2$ **(c)** $6.12 \div 6$

    (d) $16.0 \div 5$ **(e)** $54.0 \div 4$ **(f)** $3.66 \div 6$

    (g) $0.30 \div 5$ **(h)** $7.2 \div 4$ **(i)** $12.0 \div 8$

    (j) $0.45 \div 5$ **(k)** $0.020 \div 5$ **(l)** $0.20 \div 4$

3 Work out these.

    (a) $1.4 \div 7$ **(b)** $0.56 \div 8$ **(c)** $2.48 \div 4$

    (d) $1.52 \div 4$ **(e)** $7.0 \div 2$ **(f)** $0.804 \div 4$

    (g) $3.0 \div 6$ **(h)** $5.2 \div 4$ **(i)** $4.5 \div 9$

4 4 friends buy a football for £13 between them.
How much do they each pay?

5 Share £192 equally between 5 people.
How much do they each get?

6 Michelle goes on a walking holiday.
She walks these distances.

Monday	16 miles
Tuesday	10 miles
Wednesday	14 miles
Thursday	18 miles
Friday	12 miles

    (a) What is her total distance?

    (b) Humza says 'That is over 15 miles a day.'
          Is he right?

7 Look at this advert.

    (a) Six people go as a group.
          What is the cost for each person?

    (b) Meena is part of the group.
          How much does the group ticket save Meena?

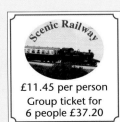

Scenic Railway

£11.45 per person
Group ticket for
6 people £37.20

Finishing off

Now that you have finished this chapter you should be able to:

● multiply a decimal by a whole number
● divide a decimal by a whole number.

Review exercise

1 Work out these.

(a) 0.5×8	**(b)** 0.2×6	**(c)** 0.3×7
(d) 0.6×4	**(e)** 0.004×2	**(f)** 0.1×12
(g) 1.5×3	**(h)** 2.7×5	**(i)** 0.72×3
(j) 0.65×4	**(k)** 1.23×6	**(l)** 1.50×4

2 Work out these.

(a) 0.1×7	**(b)** 0.02×8	**(c)** 0.003×5
(d) 0.007×2	**(e)** 0.8×2	**(f)** 0.6×7
(g) 1.503×4	**(h)** 1.63×3	**(i)** 3.95×6
(j) 4.12×9	**(k)** 6.54×8	**(l)** 0.0483×5

3 Work out these.

(a) 6.3×8	**(b)** 7.2×9	**(c)** 13.65×4
(d) 19.12×3	**(e)** 3.418×2	**(f)** 0.023×6

4 Find the total cost of these models.

	Number required	Price each
Delivery vans	3	£5.40
Cars	8	£5.45
Trucks	2	£6.75
Set of letter boxes	2	£2.84
Mail vans	5	£4.40
Taxi cab	4	£4.32

5 Find the total cost of these.

	Number required	Price each
Jigsaws	3	£12.65
Books	6	£5.72
Child's game	2	£17.28

6 Work out these.

(a) $7.2 \div 8$ (b) $6.5 \div 5$ (c) $23.5 \div 5$

(d) $3.12 \div 3$ (e) $0.564 \div 6$ (f) $0.872 \div 8$

7 Work out these.

(a) $8.7 \div 3$ (b) $0.54 \div 2$ (c) $6.4 \div 4$

(d) $0.65 \div 5$ (e) $4.10 \div 5$ (f) $9.6 \div 8$

8 A group of girls write down their ages.

| 12 | 14 | 12 | 12 | 11 | 10 | 13 | 12 |

(a) Find their total age.

(b) Find their average age.

> *Divide the total by the number of girls.*

9 A group of boys write down their ages.

| 12 | 12 | 14 | 13 | 13 | 13 | 10 | 11 | 10 |

(a) Find their total age.

(b) Find their average age.

10 Copy and complete the following crossword.

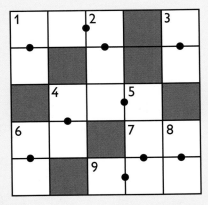

Across
1 8.1×2
4 8.9×4
6 12.8×5
7 3.25×4
9 0.43×6

Down
1 $7.2 \div 6$
2 $11.00 \div 4$
3 $23.5 \div 5$
4 $27.2 \div 8$
5 $123.0 \div 2$
6 $24.8 \div 4$
8 $26.6 \div 7$

Class 7G have another Reward lesson.

Ali

I have been working really hard.

All right, you can have another Reward lesson.

Mr Jones

Matching pairs

Ali, Karl and Mercy play **Matching pairs** with a pack of special cards.

 Look at these cards.
Pick out the matching pairs.

| 0.4 | 4% | $\frac{2}{5}$ | $\frac{1}{10}$ | $\frac{4}{100}$ | 0.1 |

All the cards are laid face down.
Then they take turns to turn over 2 cards.

I have got 2 the same. Another pair for me, and I get another turn.

0.3

$\frac{3}{10}$

 Why are some cards missing from the picture?

At the end of the game

I got 6 pairs.

I got 5 pairs.

Karl

I only got 4 pairs.

Mercy

 Who is the winner?

 Task

Play **Matching pairs** with your friends.

Dominoes

Lucy and John are playing dominoes.

John   Lucy

It is John's turn.
Here are his dominoes.

This is the game so far.

? Which dominoes can John play?

? Who is the winner in a game of dominoes?

? How do you score in dominoes?

Lucy and John change to Maths dominoes. Look at their game so far.

Here are Lucy's dominoes. Which can she play?

| 5 × 6 | 9 × 3 | | 2 × 12 | 16 | | 4 × 4 | 18 | | 3 × 4 | 12 | | 9 × 2 | 30 |

Here are Lucy's dominoes. Which can she play?

Play **Maths dominoes** with a friend.

Look at this map.
It shows the bus route of the 57A.

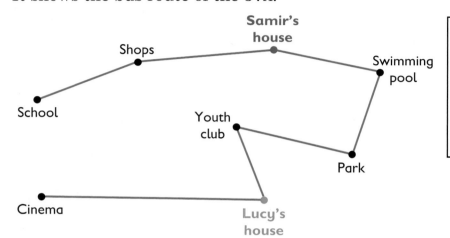

Bus 57A

20p to board bus
plus
10p for each stop

? Samir wants to go from his house to the park.
How much does this cost?

Task

I Copy the table and fill in the missing prices.

	Cinema	Park	School	Shops	Swimming pool	Youth club
Price from Samir's house		40p				
Price from Lucy's house						

2 Samir goes to a film. Then he goes swimming.
How much are his bus tickets?
Remember he must end up back at home!

You can use a **number machine** to work out the prices of the bus tickets.

Number of stops ⟶ ☓ 10 ⟶ + 20 ⟶ Price in pence

? Explain how the number machine works.

Exercise

1 Pete is going bowling with some friends. He uses a number machine to work out the cost.

Number of people → ×3 → Cost (£)

Copy and complete the table.

Number of people	2	3	4	5	6	7	10	12
Cost (£)								

2 Tim buys some CDs.

(a) Copy and complete this number machine. It works out how much Tim spends.

Number of CDs → ? → Cost (£)

All CDs only £12 each

(b) Tim buys 4 CDs. How much does he spend?

3 Ali is raising money for her youth club. She sells tickets for a party. This number machine works out how much money she raises.

Number of people → ×2 → Money raised (£)

Tickets £2 each

(a) How much money does Ali raise when she sells
  (i) 10 tickets   **(ii)** 15 tickets   **(iii)** 30 tickets?

Ali works out how many drinks to buy.

Number of tickets sold → ×2 → +1 → Number of drinks

(b) How many drinks does Ali buy when she sells
  (i) 10 tickets   **(ii)** 15 tickets   **(iii)** 30 tickets?

Using number machines

Mercy

Mobile Phones

Calls cost 10p for each minute plus 5p connection

Mercy uses a number machine to work out the cost of her call.

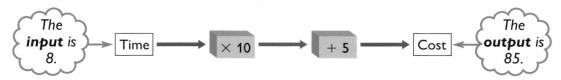

The **input** is 8. → Time → × 10 → + 5 → Cost ← The **output** is 85.

? How much is Mercy's phone call?
What do **input** and **output** mean?

Task

1 Copy and complete the table.
Use Mercy's number machine to find the missing costs.

Time (mins)	1	2	3	4	8	10	20
Cost					85p		

2 Find the outputs for these number machines.

(a) 7 → + 3 → ☐

(b) 22 → − 6 → ☐

(c) 8 → × 2 → ☐

(d) 21 → ÷ 3 → ☐

(e) 45 → − 20 → ☐

(f) 4 → × 4 → ☐

(g) 12 → + 9 → ☐

(h) 81 → ÷ 9 → ☐

Match your answers to the letters to crack the code.

W	25	E	3	P	4	R	21	O	16

L	15	D	7	A	6	K	9	G	10

? Is this number machine the same as Mercy's?

Input → + 5 → × 10 → Output

Exercise

1 Find the outputs for each of these number machines.

(a) [4] ⟶ [+ 9] ⟶ [ ]

(b) [19] ⟶ [− 12] ⟶ [ ]

(c) [36] ⟶ [÷ 3] ⟶ [ ]

2 Look at this number machine.

[Input] ⟶ [+ 3] ⟶ [Output]

Copy and complete the table.

Input	1	2	3	4	5	10	20
Output							

3 Find the outputs for each of these number machines.

(a) [4] ⟶ [× 3] ⟶ [+ 1] ⟶ [ ]

(b) [3] ⟶ [× 2] ⟶ [− 1] ⟶ [ ]

(c) [2] ⟶ [× 4] ⟶ [+ 3] ⟶ [ ]

4 Mercy sees an advert from another mobile phone company.

Mobile Phones
Calls cost 5p
for each minute plus
3p connection

(a) Copy and complete the number machine.

[Time (minutes)] ⟶ [×   ] ⟶ [+   ] ⟶ [Cost (pence)]

(b) Copy the table and fill in the missing numbers.

Time (mins)	1	2	3	4	5	6	7
Cost							

Using a rule

Harry and Michelle are playing the **Number machine game**.
Harry thinks of a number machine.
Michelle wants to find his rule.
She tries different inputs.

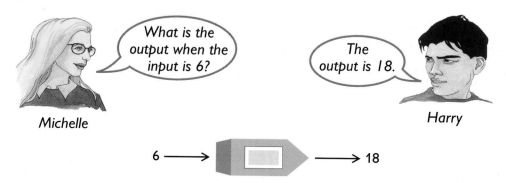

Michelle

> What is the output when the input is 6?

> The output is 18.

Harry

6 ⟶ [▢] ⟶ 18

? **Find a rule for Harry's number machine.**
Now find another rule.
How many rules can you find?

Task

I Find the rules for these number machines.

(a) 4 ⟶ [+ ▭] ⟶ 10   **(b)** 21 ⟶ [− ▭] ⟶ 17

(c) 13 ⟶ [+ ▭] ⟶ 27   **(d)** 42 ⟶ [− ▭] ⟶ 17

2 Find the rules for these number machines.

(a) 3 ⟶ [× ▭] ⟶ 12   **(b)** 24 ⟶ [÷ ▭] ⟶ 12

(c) 10 ⟶ [× ▭] ⟶ 50   **(d)** 35 ⟶ [÷ ▭] ⟶ 7

3 Play the **Number machine game** with a partner.

? **How many rules can you find for this number machine?**

4 ⟶ [▭ ⟶ ▭] ⟶ 15

Exercise

1 These number machines use **adding** and **subtracting**.
Find the rules.

(a) 5 ⟶ ▢ ⟶ 8   **(b)** 14 ⟶ ▢ ⟶ 9

(c) 17 ⟶ ▢ ⟶ 32   **(d)** 46 ⟶ ▢ ⟶ 29

2 These number machines use **multiplying** and **dividing**.
Find the rules.

(a) 2 ⟶ ▢ ⟶ 10   **(b)** 20 ⟶ ▢ ⟶ 5

(c) 42 ⟶ ▢ ⟶ 6   **(d)** 9 ⟶ ▢ ⟶ 54

3 Tim is playing the **Number machine game**.

Input ⟶ ▢ ⟶ Output

Here is a table of inputs and outputs for the number machine.

Input	1	2	3	4	5
Output	3	4	5	6	7

What rule is the number machine using?

4 Avonford cinema uses a number machine to work out the costs
of tickets.

Number of adults
or Number of children ⟶ ▢ ⟶ Price

Our tickets cost £12.

So did ours.

(a) What rule is the number machine using for **adult** tickets?
(b) What rule is the number machine using for **child** tickets?

Finishing off

Now that you have finished this chapter you should be able to:

- understand the terms **number machine**, **input** and **output**
- find the output of a number machine
- find the rule a number machine is using.

Review exercise

SU

1 Roger is a taxi driver.
His meter uses this number machine to work out the fare.

Number of miles ⟶ × 30 ⟶ + 70 ⟶ Price in pence

Copy the table and fill in the missing costs.

Number of miles	1	2	3	4	5	6	10
Fare (p)			160				
Fare (£)			£1.60				

2 Find the outputs for each of these number machines.

(a) 32 ⟶ − 17 ⟶ ☐

(b) 27 ⟶ + 8 ⟶ ☐

(c) 40 ⟶ ÷ 5 ⟶ ☐

(d) 5 ⟶ × 3 ⟶ ☐

(e) 12 ⟶ + 5 ⟶ − 3 ⟶ ☐

(f) 8 ⟶ × 2 ⟶ ÷ 4 ⟶ ☐

(g) 7 ⟶ × 2 ⟶ + 5 ⟶ ☐

(h) 5 ⟶ + 19 ⟶ ÷ 6 ⟶ ☐

3 At Avonford park you can hire a rowing boat.

ROW-A-BOAT

£6 for each hour + £10 deposit

(a) Copy and complete this number machine.

Number of hours ⟶ × ☐ ⟶ + ☐ ⟶ Cost in pounds

(b) Copy and complete the table.

Time (hours)	1	2	3	4	6	8	10
Cost (£)							

4 Look at this number machine.

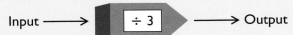

Input ⟶ ÷ 3 ⟶ Output

Copy this table and fill in the missing numbers.

Input	3	6	9	30	63
Output					

5 Look at this number machine.

Input ⟶ ☐ ⟶ Output

(a) Here is a table of inputs and outputs for the number machine.

Input	1	2	3	4	5
Output	2	4	6	8	10

What rule is the number machine using?

(b) Look at these tables of inputs and outputs for other number machines.
What rule is each number machine using?

(i)

Input	3	6	11	14	19
Output	1	4	9	12	17

(ii)

Input	5	10	15	20	25
Output	1	2	3	4	5

15 Scale drawing

Scale

A shop sells toy train sets for 3–5 year olds.
There are different sizes.
The small set is exactly half the size of the standard set.
The **scale**, small set : standard set, is **1 : 2**.

Say this as 'I to 2'

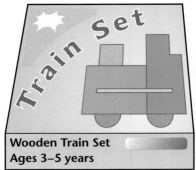

Wooden Train Set
Ages 3–5 years

 Complete this sentence.

The standard set is [ ] the size of the small set.

 What is the scale, standard set to small set?

Task

1 The track in the small set is a circle, 30 cm diameter.

   (a) What shape is the track in the standard set?
   (b) How far across is it?

2 This is an accurate drawing of the train from the small set.

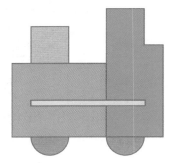

   (a) How long is the train?
   (b) How tall is the train?
   (c) Make an accurate drawing of the train from the standard set.

3 The shop also sells a giant sized train set.
   It is 10 times bigger than the standard set.

   (a) How long is the giant train?
   (b) How tall is it?
      Can children ride on it?

 What is the scale of the small set to the giant set?

Exercise

1. This is a photograph of Tim's goldfish, Spot.

   (a) How long is Spot in the photograph?

   In real life, Spot is 12 cm long.

   (b) What is the scale of the photograph?
   (c) How wide is Spot's tail in the photograph?
   (d) How wide is Spot's tail in real life?

2. Three sorts of creatures live on the planet Grunge: zats, humans and blobbits.

   The creatures look like this.

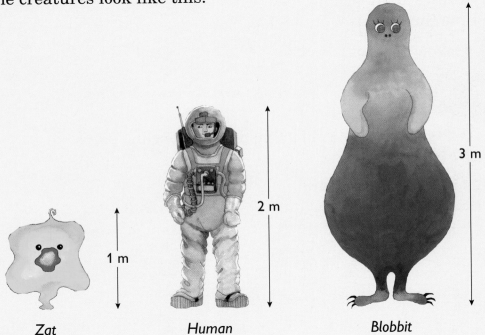

Zat — 1 m   Human — 2 m   Blobbit — 3 m

   Find these scales.

   (a) The height of a human : The height of a blobbit.
   (b) The height of a blobbit : The height of a zat.
   (c) The height of a zat : The height of a human.

   The width of a zat is 1 metre.
   The width of a zat : The width of a blobbit is 2 : 3.

   (d) What is the width of a blobbit?

Activity Find out what scales are used for model trains, cars or aeroplanes.
Make a poster to show what you find.

Scale drawing

Harry draws a plan of his bedroom.

? Measure Harry's plan.

The scale of the plan is **1 cm to 1 m**.

? How long is Harry's bedroom?
How wide is it?

? Do you think **1 cm to 1 m** is a good
scale to use? Why?

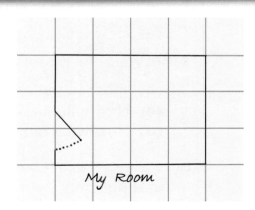

Harry draws another plan.
This time the scale is **4 cm to 1 m**.

? How long is his new plan? How wide is it?

Task

1 Using the scale 4 cm to 1 m, draw an outline plan of Harry's bedroom on
graph paper.

This is Harry's furniture.

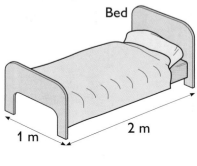

Bed

Wardrobe

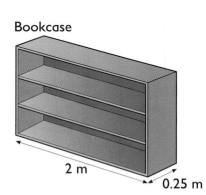

Bookcase

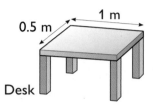

Desk

2 Use the same scale to draw shapes of the furniture.

3 Cut these out and arrange them on the plan.

? On Harry's new plan the window is 10 cm wide.
How wide is the real window?

Exercise

1 This is a plan of Harry's garden.

Scale 1 cm to 2 m

(a) How long is the real path?
(b) How long is the real pond?
(c) What are the real measurements of the shed?
(d) How far is it from the back door to the tree?

2 Harry's mum is buying a new kitchen.
The salesman has drawn a plan for her with a scale of **5 cm to 1 m**.

(a) On the plan, the length of the kitchen is 25 cm.
What is the length of the real kitchen?
(b) The real kitchen is 4 m wide.
How wide is the kitchen on the plan?
(c) The window on the plan is 7.5 cm wide.
How wide is the real window?
(d) The real work surface is 50 cm wide.
How wide is it on the plan?

Activity Draw an outline plan of a room in your house.
Make cut-outs for the main pieces of furniture in the room.
Use the plan and the cut outs to re-design the layout of the room.

Map scales

Christina and Karl spend a day at Avonford Theme Park.

This map of part of the Park has a scale of **1 cm to 50 metres**.
This means that every centimetre on the map represents 50 metres in real life.

The real life distance is   Map distance (in cm) × 50 metres.

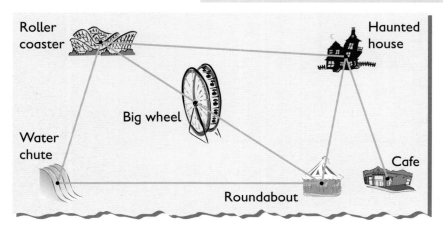

 How far is it from the cafe to the Haunted House in the real Park?

Task

Christina and Karl go round the Park. They have a go on each ride.

1 Measure the distances then work out how far it is between each ride.
Draw a table like this to help you.
The first distance has already been put in.

Rides	Distance on plan	Distance in Park
Roller coaster to Big wheel	3 cm	150 m

Christina and Karl want to go on each ride by walking the shortest distance.

2 Work out the shortest tour.
How far do they walk altogether?

From the Haunted House to the Car Park is 550 metres.

 How far is this distance on the map?

Exercise

Pete the Pirate has buried all his treasure on Nuku Island.
This is Pete's map of the island.

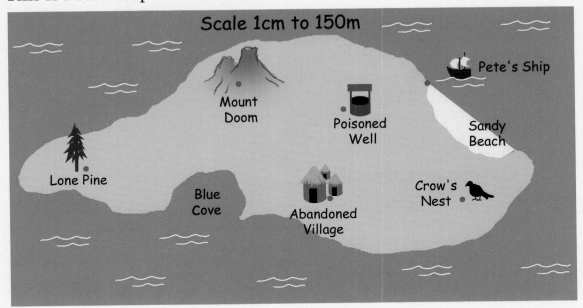

1 How long is the sandy beach?

2 How wide is Blue Cove?

3 How far is it from the lone pine to the crow's nest?

4 Pete walked from his ship to the top of Mount Doom, then down to the abandoned village.
How far did Pete walk?

5 The treasure is buried exactly 1050 metres from the poisoned well.
The treasure is not in the sea.
Where did Pete bury the treasure?

Activity **1** Find examples of these maps.

(a) An A–Z **(b)** A driver's road map
(c) An Ordnance survey map **(d)** An atlas

2 What is the scale for each map?

3 Use the scales to work out the distance across a page of each map.

Finishing off

Review exercise

1   The scale on a plan is **1 cm to 20 m**.

   (a) What are the real distances shown on the plan by
   (i) 4 cm   **(ii)** 2.5 cm   **(iii)** 6 cm   **(iv)** 10.5 cm?

   (b) What measurements on the plan show real distances of
   (i) 60 m   **(ii)** 50 m   **(iii)** 140 m?

2   A model car is made to a scale of **1 : 50**.

The model is 5 cm long.

(a) How long is the real car?

The wheel on the real car is 75 cm across.

(b) How far across is the wheel on the model car?

3 A map of Mark's town is drawn to a scale of **1 cm to 100 m**.
This is part of the map.

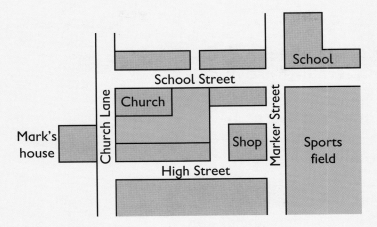

Mark walks to school from his house, past the church.

(a) How far does he walk to school?

He walks home from school past the shop.

(b) How far does he walk to get home?
(c) Which is the shortest route and by how much?

Activity

1 Measure in centimetres

   (a) your height
   (b) the length of your arms
   (c) the length of your legs
   (d) the width of your shoulders.

2 Choose a suitable scale and draw a scale drawing of yourself wearing your favourite clothes.

3 When everyone has finished their drawings, put them all together on a poster for the whole class.

The mode

Megan and her friends are going on a trip.
They all vote for their favourite activity.

Activity	Frequency
Theme park	7
Cinema	4
Bowling	8
Skating	5
Aqua park	6

 Which is the most popular activity?

The most popular is called the **mode**.

At the bowling alley they hire shoes.
This frequency table shows their shoe sizes.

Shoe size	Frequency
5	4
6	11
7	9
8	6

 What is the mode of the shoe sizes?

Task

Collect the shoe sizes for your class.
Copy this table and use it to record your results.

Shoe size	Frequency

? **What is the mode of the shoe sizes for your class?**

Draw a bar chart to show the shoe sizes for your class.

? **How do you find the mode from a bar chart?**

? **How do you find the mode from a frequency table?**

Exercise

1 Find the mode of each of these sets of numbers.

(a) 3, 4, 4, 6, 7, 7, 8, 8, 8, 9
(b) 11, 13, 14, 14, 14, 15, 15, 15, 15, 20

2 Jack does a survey of the pocket money of members of his class. Here are his results.

Amount	Frequency
£2	10
£2.25	6
£2.50	5
£3	7
£3.50	2

Jack says that the average pocket money is £2.

(a) Why has Jack chosen £2?
(b) Do you agree with Jack?
        Give a reason for your answer.

3

The rose is still Britain's favourite flower

Humza decides to test this claim.
He asks 20 people at a garden centre to choose their favourite flower.
Here are his results.

rose	daffodil	primrose	rose	rose
primrose	rose	lily	lily	daffodil
carnation	carnation	rose	primrose	lily
lily	rose	carnation	lily	rose

(a) Make a frequency table of Humza's results.
(b) What is the mode?
(c) Does this agree with the claim?

Activity

Britain's favourite pet is the dog.

Conduct a survey to find the favourite pet in your class.
Do your results agree with the claim?

The mean

Here are Karl's and Alan's bowling scores.

6 6 26 8 22 7 5 8 9 23

26 4 30 7 8 5 12 7 9

Karl

Alan

 Who is the better bowler?
Give a reason for your answer.

Task

1 Add up Karl's scores

$6 + 6 + 26 + 8 + 22 + 7 + 5 + 8 + 9 + 23 =$

2 Divide this number by 10. ← *There are 10 scores.*

Average score = ——————

=

*This type of average is called the **mean**.*

3 Work out Alan's mean score.  *Alan only has 9 scores.*

4 Who has the higher mean score, Alan or Karl?

 Look at Karl's and Alan's scores again.
What is Karl's mode score?
What is Alan's mode score?

 You want to compare Karl's and Alan's scores.
Which is better, the mode or the mean?

Exercise

1 Work out the mean of these sets of numbers.

(a) 3, 4, 6, 7, 8, 8   **(b)** 3, 3, 5, 6, 7, 9, 9, 10, 12, 12

(c) 7, 18, 22, 34, 40   **(d)** 2, 2, 6, 7, 10, 19, 19, 25

2 Ali has measured the heights of her friends.
Here are her results.

Christina	135 cm	Meena	142 cm	Kim	154 cm
Mercy	146 cm	Sophie	150 cm	Megan	139 cm
Lucy	159 cm	Michelle	147 cm		

Work out the mean height.

3 Tim sees this label on a packet of nails.
He counts the number of nails in
10 packets.
Here are his results.

21, 24, 26, 22, 27, 27, 28,
26, 24, 23

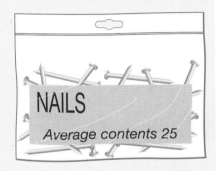

NAILS

Average contents 25

(a) Work out the mean number of nails in these packets.
(b) Do you agree with the label? Explain your answer.

4 Jo is a keen swimmer.
Her average time for the 100 m
breaststroke is 32 seconds.
Her personal best is 31 seconds.
She records her times for the next
12 training sessions.

33, 32, 32, 34, 32, 32, 31,
33, 31, 31, 32, 31

(a) Work out her mean time.
(b) Is Jo getting better?

Activity   Measure the heights of everyone in your class.
Work out the mean height.

The median

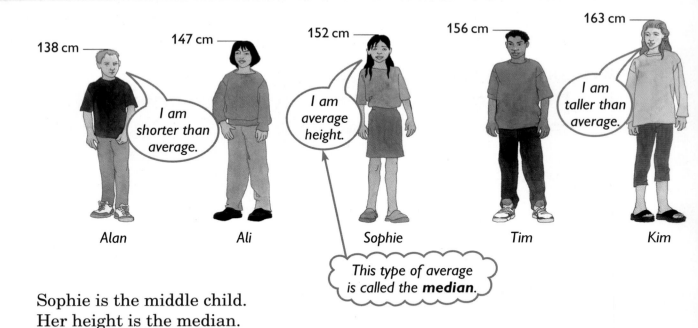

Sophie is the middle child.
Her height is the median.

 What is the median height?

Task

The table shows the normal life span of some pets.

1 **(a)** Write the list in order of the life spans.
   (b) Which pet has the median life span?
   (c) What is the median life span?
   (d) Explain why the life span of a guinea pig is below average.

2 **(a)** Think of some more pets.
       Find out their normal life spans.
       Add these pets to your list.
   (b) What is the median for your new list?
   (c) Which pet has the median life span?

Pet	Life span
Cat	15 years
Small dog	12 years
Large dog	10 years
Hamster	4 years
Guinea pig	7 years

There are 3 types of averages. What are they?

Explain how to find each one.

Exercise

1 Write down the median for each of these sets of numbers.

(a) 2, 3, 5, 5, 7, 8, 10   (b) 18, 20, 21, 24, 27, 30, 30, 31, 39
(c) 124, 136, 176, 189, 190   (d) 1.2, 1.7, 2.1, 3.9, 5.0

2 (i) Write these sets of numbers in order.
(ii) Find the median number.

(a) 5, 3, 7, 9, 11, 2, 10   (b) 12, 15, 11, 21, 12, 17, 22, 15, 19

3

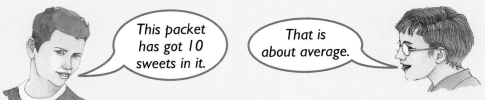

This packet has got 10 sweets in it.

That is about average.

Shop assistant

Pete

Pete counts the number of sweets in 15 packets.
Here are his results.

9, 12, 10, 10, 14, 9, 8, 11, 11, 12, 10, 13, 10, 12, 11

(a) Find the median number of sweets in a packet.
(b) Does Pete's packet contain an average number of sweets?

4 The table shows the hours of sunshine at Brightsea and Coveton for a week in August.

	Mon	Tues	Weds	Thur	Fri	Sat	Sun
Brightsea	7	2	5	10	9	9	10
Coveton	6	3	4	11	11	8	12

(a) Find the median hours of sunshine for
   (i) Brightsea   (ii) Coveton.
(b) Which town has more sunshine? Explain your answer.

Activity **1** This list does not have a middle number.

5, 6, 6, 7, 9, 10, 12, 15

(a) Write down the middle 2 numbers.
(b) Find the number half way between them.

You have found the median value. It is 8.

2 Find the median of these sets of numbers.

(a) 4, 5, 7, 8   (b) 10, 12, 13, 15, 16, 18

Finishing off

Now that you have finished this chapter you should:

- be able to find the mean, median and mode of a set of data
- know that they are all types of averages.

Review exercise

1 Find the mode of these sets of numbers.

(a) 34, 35, 35, 37, 37, 37, 38, 39
(b) 1, 3, 5, 2, 1, 2, 5, 2

2 Find the median of these sets of numbers.

(a) 8, 10, 11, 12, 12
(b) 27, 2, 13, 41, 19, 12, 17

3 Calculate the mean of these sets of numbers.

(a) 3, 5, 6, 8, 10, 10
(b) 12, 4, 7, 2, 10, 11, 15, 5, 7, 8

4 Here are the goals scored by Avonford Town in 10 matches.

1, 2, 2, 0, 3, 1, 1, 1, 2, 3

Work out the goal average.

> This is the mean.

5 Mark wants to know which is the most popular type of car in his town.
He writes down the makes of the cars passing his school.
Here is his list.

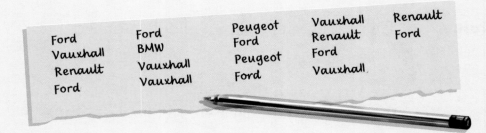

Ford
Vauxhall
Renault
Ford

Ford
BMW
Vauxhall
Vauxhall

Peugeot
Ford
Peugeot
Ford

Vauxhall
Renault
Ford
Vauxhall

Renault
Ford

(a) Make a frequency table to show the number of each type of car.
(b) Find the mode from your table.

6 These sets of numbers do not have a middle number.
Find the median of each set.

   (a) 12, 14, 15, 17, 21, 22
   (b) 22, 23, 25, 26, 28, 31, 31, 33

7 Mr Jones and Mrs Brown want to compare how long it takes them
to get to work.
They write down their journey times each day.

	Time in minutes						
	Mon	**Tues**	**Weds**	**Thur**	**Fri**	**Sat**	**Sun**
Mr Jones	15	22	16	22	25	–	–
Mrs Brown	16	17	24	21	25	26	18

   (a) Find the median time for
      (i) Mr Jones   **(ii)** Mrs Brown.
   (b) Calculate the mean time for
      (i) Mr Jones   **(ii)** Mrs Brown.
   (c) Who has the shorter average journey time?
   (d) Which average have you used?

Activity

Samir has counted the lengths of the first 50 words in his
reading book.

Here are his results.

Number of letters	Frequency
1	5
2	7
3	10
4	17
5	5
More than 5	6

 What is the mode for these data?

Choose 50 words from a book of your own.
Find the mode for the word lengths from your book.
Compare the word lengths in your book with your friends.
Is it the same for all books?

? In the football league, how many points does a team get for a win?
What about a draw? What if they lose?

? Look at Bolton's results. How many matches have they played?
How many points have they got?

Team	Played	Won	Drawn	Lost	Points
Bolton Wanderers		4	2	1	

Task

Avonford Ladies Football Club play in a league.

> 3 points for a win,
> 1 for a draw,
> 0 for losing.

1 Copy this table and fill in the missing numbers.

Team	Played	Won	Drawn	Lost	Points
Avonford		9	2	1	
Shellbury		8	2	2	
Eastpool		6	1	4	
Bannington	11	5	3		
Churchton	10		0		18

2 Bingsley have 11 points from 12 games.
Copy this table and fill it in four different ways.

Team	Played	Won	Drawn	Lost	Points
Bingsley	12				11

? How do you work out 'Played'?
What formula do you use?

? How do you work out 'Points'?
What formula do you use?

> You have used
> two formulae on
> this page.

Exercise

1 **(a)** What is the cost of
   (i) 10 litres
   (ii) 20 litres
   (iii) 100 litres of petrol?

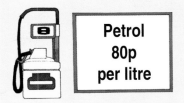

Petrol
80p
per litre

(b) Copy and complete this formula.

cost in pence = number of litres ×

2

How many miles away is the lightning?

Start counting with the lightning. Stop when you hear the thunder. Then divide by 5.

Jack   Jack's mum

(a) **(i)** Jack counts to 15.
          How many miles away is the lightning?
     (ii) Karl gets to 1.
          How many miles away is the lightning?

(b) Copy and complete this formula.

distance =   ÷ 5

3

Sardines
25p

Mackerel
30p

Tuna
50p

(a) Work out the cost of

   (i) 2 tins of sardines, 2 tins of mackerel and 1 tin of tuna
   (ii) 4 tins of sardines and 5 tins of tuna
   (iii) 1 of each tin.

(b) Copy and complete this formula.

cost in pence = 25 × number of tins of sardines

+ 30 × number of tins of

+   ×

Using formulae

Avonford Theme Park

Adults £8
Children £4

How much will it cost for all of us?

Wayne writes:

> Cost (£) = 8 × number of adults + 4 × number of children
> Cost (£) = 8 × 2 + 4 × 3

*This is a **formula**.*

 How much does it cost for Wayne's family?

Task

1 This table shows the costs for different groups at the Park.
Copy the table and fill in the missing numbers.

		Number of children			
		0	1	2	3
Number of adults	0	£0			
	1			£16	
	2				£28
	3		£28		

It costs £28 for 2 adults and 3 children.

2 Look at this receipt.

Avonford Theme Park

Adults
Children

Total £40

How many adults and children are there in the group?
Find as many answers as you can.

 Avonford Theme Park is having a special offer.

£2 off all tickets!

Write down a formula for the cost (in £) of a group.

Exercise

1 Jo is planning a party.
She uses a formula to work out how many bottles of cola to buy.

> Number of bottles of cola = 2 × number of people + 10

Work out how many bottles she buys for
(a) 10   **(b)** 20   **(c)** 50 people.

2 Look at this formula.

> Price (£) = 2 × number of fish
>   + number of portions of chips

Today's Special

Fish £2 Chips £

(a) Work out the cost of
     (i)   3 fish and 4 portions of chips
     (ii)   4 fish and 5 portions of chips
     (iii) 2 fish.

(b) How much is one portion of chips?

3 Look at this advert.

     SPEEDY BOATS
     £5 per hour

(a) Copy and complete this formula.

> Cost of hire (£) =   × number of hours

(b) Work out the cost to hire a boat for
     (i)   2 hours   **(ii)** 3 hours   **(iii)** 12 hours.

4 Alan is planning a trip for his
youth group.

Avonford films	
Adults	£5
Children	£2

(a) Copy and complete this formula.

> Cost (£) =   × number of adults +   × number of children

(b) Work out the cost for
     (i)   2 adults and 10 children
     (ii)   3 adults and 15 children
     (iii) 1 adult and 4 children.

(c) The trip costs £30.
How many adults and children are there?
Find as many answers as you can.

Working backwards

Look at this number pyramid.

The number in the top brick is found using this formula.

Number in top brick = Number in red brick × Number in blue brick

Megan writes:

Number in red brick × 4 = 24
    Number in red brick = 24 ÷ 4
50   Number in red brick = 6

*To undo '× by 4'
I must '÷ by 4'.*

Megan

 Why does Megan's method work?

Task

1 Look at this number pyramid.

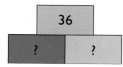

What are the numbers in the red and blue bricks?
Find as many whole number answers as you can.

2 Look at this number pyramid.

Copy and complete this table.

Red Brick	1	2	3							
Blue Brick							8	6	4	

? **What are the missing numbers here?**

(a) ☐ + 7 = 12 **(b)** ☐ − 9 = 21 **(c)** ☐ ÷ 6 = 3

? **How did you work out your answers?**

Exercise

1 Copy these sums and find the missing numbers.

(a) ☐ $+ 5 = 17$ (b) ☐ $+ 9 = 15$

(c) ☐ $- 7 = 14$ (d) ☐ $- 15 = 17$

(e) ☐ $+ 12 = 24$ (f) ☐ $- 10 = 11$

(g) $13 +$ ☐ $= 25$ (h) ☐ $\times 4 = 20$

(i) ☐ $\times 7 = 56$ (j) ☐ $\div 3 = 7$

(k) ☐ $\div 8 = 4$ (l) ☐ $\times 9 = 63$

W 5	T 7	D 12	H 8	E 21	A 32	R 6

Match your answers to the letters to answer the question.
What is a vampire's favourite breakfast?

2 The cost of buying packets of crisps at the shops is:

> Cost (in pence) = 20 × number of packets of crisps

Mercy buys some crisps.
Work out how many packets of crisps she buys when she spends

(a) 40p   (b) 60p   (c) £1   (d) £1.60.

3 Pete is building a fence.
He uses these formulae.

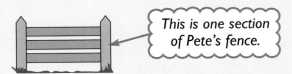

This is one section of Pete's fence.

> Number of posts = number of sections + 1
> Number of bars = 3 × number of sections

(a) Work out how many **posts** Pete needs for
   (i) 2 sections   (ii) 3 sections
   (iii) 4 sections   (iv) 5 sections.

(b) Work out how many bars Pete needs for
   (i) 2 sections   (ii) 3 sections
   (iii) 4 sections   (iv) 5 sections.

(c) How many **sections** does Pete build when he uses
   (i) 7 posts   (ii) 8 posts
   (iii) 10 posts   (iv) 20 posts?

(d) How many **sections** does Pete build when he uses
   (i) 18 bars   (ii) 21 bars
   (iii) 30 bars   (iv) 42 bars?

Finishing off

Now that you have finished this chapter you should:

- understand what a formula is
- know how to use a formula
- be able to work backwards using a formula.

Review exercise

1 What is the cost of

(a) 3 litres
(b) 4 litres
(c) 10 litres of lemonade?

Special offer!

Lemonade
only
30p per litre

2 Look at this advert.

(a) Complete this formula.

Price = [　　　] × number of CDs

+ [　　　] × number of DVDs

Mad about Music

CDs £12 each
DVDs £15 each

(b) Work out the price of
(i) 3 CDs
(ii) 2 DVDs
(iii) 2 CDs and 1 DVD
(iv) 4 CDs and 3 DVDs.

3 Look at this advert.

(a) Complete this formula.

Cost (in pence) = [　　　] × number of minutes

Mobile Phones
Calls cost 25p per minute

(b) Work out how long John and Humza each spent on the phone.

I was charged £2.75.

John

My calls cost £5.25.

Humza

4 Find the missing numbers.

Across

3 ☐ + 6 = 19

5 9 − ☐ = 8

7 4 × ☐ = 32

9 27 ÷ ☐ = 3

11 ☐ − 4 = 1

Down

1 12 ÷ ☐ = 3

2 ☐ × 3 = 21

3 9 × ☐ = 18

4 5 × ☐ = 15

6 24 − ☐ = 15

8 7 + ☐ = 17

10 5 × ☐ = 30

Copy this grid.
Use your answers to the clues
to fill it in.

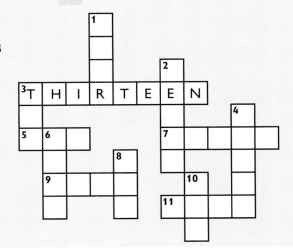

Investigation

Samir has a formula for estimating the height of a person.

Measure round your head. Multiply your answer by 3. This gives your height.

Samir

How tall am I?

Becky

1 How tall is Becky?

2 How tall are these people?

3 Does Samir's formula work?
Measure yourself and some friends to find out.

Pete and Lucy are playing snakes and ladders.
Pete writes down the moves.

Pete

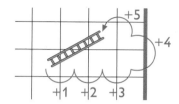

This ladder is + 5.

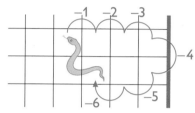

This snake is − 6.

Lucy

Task

Copy and complete this table to show Pete's moves. He starts at 0.

Die	Snake or ladder	Total	Square
3	+12	15	15
4	−	4	19
1			39
3			24
4			45
5	−		
3			92
1			75
6			
4	−		

```
99  98  97  96  95  94  93  92  91  90
END
80  81  82  83  84  85  86  87  88  89
79  78  77  76  75  74  73  72  71  70
60  61  62  63  64  65  66  67  68  69
59  58  57  56  55  54  53  52  51  50
40  41  42  43  44  45  46  47  48  49
39  38  37  36  35  34  33  32  31  30
20  21  22  23  24  25  26  27  28  29
19  18  17  16  15  14  13  12  11  10
0   1   2   3   4   5   6   7   8   9
START
```

You can show moves on a straight line.

Here are +5 (right)

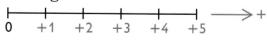

and (−6) (left) −

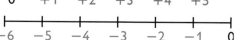

? **Show +5 followed by (−6) on this number line.**

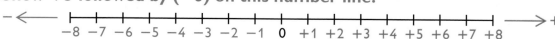

Exercise

SU

1 Copy and complete this number line.

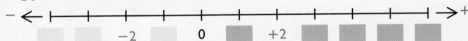

SU

2 Copy this number line.
Place these numbers on your line.

−4, +6, −9, −7, +4

−← ┤┼┼┼┼┼┼┼┼┼┼┼┼┼┼┼┼┼┼┼├ →+
    −10   −5   0   +5   +10

3 Would you think of these as + or − numbers?

(a) A present of £5   **(b)** A debt of £2
(c) A bill for £10   **(d)** A payment to an account of £3
(e) A withdrawal from an account of £30

4 Temperatures are measured above and below zero.
Write down these temperatures. Use + or −.

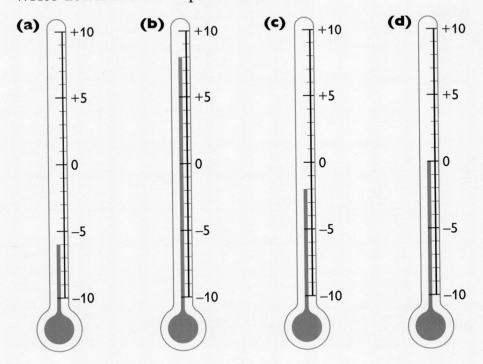

5 Write these numbers in order, smallest first.

+2, −1, −3, 0, +3, −2

Adding negative numbers

Ali and Meena play a game using two dice, one red and one blue.
They each throw both dice and move the counter along a number line.
The red score is + (to the right). The blue score is − (to the left).

So red 4 (+4) and then blue 6 (−6) looks like this.

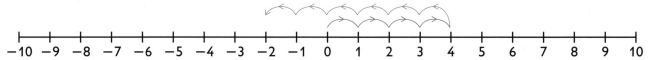

 Write these as + or − numbers.

(a)

(b)

(c)

(d)

(e)

(f)

If the counter gets to +10, Ali wins. If it gets to −10, Meena wins.

Task

Play the game with a friend.

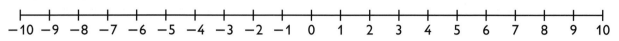

? **Who is more likely to win, Ali or Meena?**
Is the game fair?

Exercise

1 What numbers are

(a) (i) 4 more than 5   (ii) 4 less than 5
(b) (i) 3 more than 3   (ii) 3 less than 3
(c) (i) 8 more than 7   (ii) 8 less than 7
(d) (i) 10 more than 3   (ii) 10 less than 3?

2 Write these questions using + and − numbers.
Take West as − numbers and East as + numbers and work out where the finishing point is each time.

(a) West 4 and then East 3   (b) East 1 and then West 6
(c) East 3, East 4 and then West 5 (d) East 3 and then East 2
(e) West 2 and then West 1   (f) West 1 and then West 7

3 Use a number line to work out these.

(a) $(+3) + (-2)$ (b) $(-5) + (-1)$
(c) $(-3) + (+1)$ (d) $(-1) + (-2)$
(e) $(+4) + (-6)$ (f) $(-3) + (-6)$

Remember to start each question at zero.

4 What numbers are

(a) (i) $(+3) + (+2)$ (ii) $(+3) + (-2)$
(b) (i) $(+5) + (+5)$ (ii) $(+5) + (-5)$
(c) (i) $(+6) + (+8)$ (ii) $(+6) + (-8)$
(d) (i) $(+2) + (+10)$ (ii) $(+2) + (-10)$

5 Work out these.

(a) $(+9) + (-4)$ (b) $(-7) + (+3)$
(c) $(+20) + (+4) + (-18)$ (d) $(-11) + (-5)$
(e) $(-8) + (-14)$ (f) $(+5) + (-3) + (-7)$

Finishing off

Now that you have finished this chapter you should be able to:

- place a number on a number line
- write positive and negative numbers in order of size
- add positive and negative numbers.

Review exercise

1 Copy the number line below and mark on these numbers.

$$-3 \quad -5 \quad +1 \quad -1$$

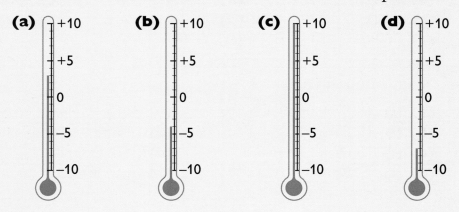

2 Use + and − numbers to write down these temperatures.

(a) **(b)** **(c)** **(d)**

3 Copy and complete the table.

Temperature in morning (°C)	Change in temperature (°C)	Temperature in afternoon (°C)
+4	Up 2	
+3	Down 4	
−1	Up 5	
−2	Down 3	
−10	Up 8	
−3	Down 1	
0	Down 4	
+1		+5
−2		−3

4 Use a number line to find

(a) $(+1) + (-2)$　　(b) $(+5) + (-3)$
(c) $(-3) + (-2)$　　(d) $(-3) + (+4)$
(e) $(-6) + (+1)$　　(f) $(-4) + (-3)$
(g) $(-5) + (+5)$　　(h) $(-4) + (+3)$
(i) $(-4) + (-2)$　　(j) $(-5) + (+6)$
(k) $(+2) + (+7)$　　(l) $(-1) + (-3) + (-4)$.

Activity

Wayne's Dad is opening his post.

 *Auntie has sent me a cheque for £60!*

 *Oh dear! Here is the bill from the garage. I must pay £285.*

He sorts out his finances on this account sheet.

Credits (+)	Debits (−)	Balance (£)
		503.00
+60.00		
	−285.00	

In this row the balance will be 503.00 + 60.00.

1 Copy the table and fill in the two missing balances.

2 Extend your copy of the account sheet.
Write these in the correct column.

(a) Payment for TV licence £9
(b) Payment for mortgage £250
(c) Payment for gas bill £70 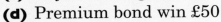　*What happens now?*
(d) Premium bond win £50
(e) Salary £1500

 *What is a mortgage?*

Work out the balance each time.

Look at this fruit pastilles packet.
Its shape is a **cuboid**.

This picture does not
show all the faces,
edges or vertices.

Vertex.

Edge.

Face

 **What is the shape of each face?**
How many faces does a cuboid have?

 **How many vertices does a cuboid have?**

 **How many edges meet at a vertex?**

 **How many edges does a cuboid have?**

Task

You are going to make a cuboid.
Look at this **net** of a cuboid.

Use
centimetre
squared
paper.

1 Copy the net and cut it out.

2 Fold the dashed lines to make the
solid cuboid.

To glue the edges together you need **flaps**.

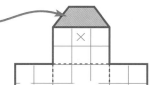

3 Decide where your net needs flaps.
Mark these edges with a cross.

4 Make a copy of your net.
Draw on flaps where you need them.

5 Cut out the new net with its flaps.

6 Glue the edges to make a cuboid.

Save your cuboid for the next lesson.

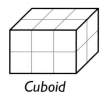

Cuboid

 Do all cuboids have the same number of faces, edges
and vertices as each other?

Exercise

1 **(a)** Use centimetre squared paper to draw the net for this cuboid.

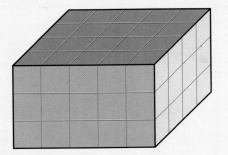

length 5 cm
width 4 cm
height 3 cm

(b) Add flaps and cut out the net.
(c) Construct the cuboid.

2 Look at this net of a **cube**.

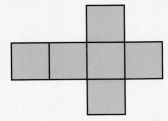

(a) What can you say about the faces of a cube?
(b) Use squared paper to draw a net of a cube.
(c) Construct the cube from your net.

Activity

Draw the net on the opposite page **on plain paper**.
Use a ruler and set square.

Cut out your net and see if the cuboid looks right.

How accurate are your right angles?

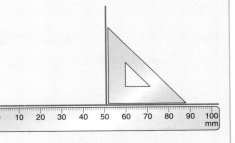

Activity

Make a box to hold 10 floppy discs.

First measure the size of **one** disc.
Then calculate the dimensions of a stack of 10 discs.

Draw the net on some thin card.
Make the dimensions be whole centimetres.
Don't forget flaps for sticking.

 Why does the box have to be slightly over-size?

Decorate the outside of your box **before** you glue the edges.

Prisms

Look at these solid shapes.

1

2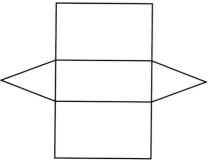

Look at these nets.

A

B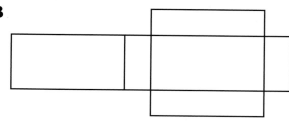

 Which net makes which shape?

These solid shapes are called **prisms**.

 Describe a prism to a friend.

Task

1 Cut out a net to make a triangular prism. Fold and glue the net to make the prism.

2 Repeat this for a pentagonal prism.

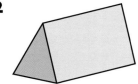 Pentagon.

3 For each prism count the number of
(a) faces   **(b)** edges   **(c)** vertices.

Do the same for your cuboid from the last lesson.
Copy and complete the table below.

Shape	Number of faces	Number of vertices	Number of edges
Triangular prism	5		
Cuboid	6	8	12
Pentagonal prism			

 What other everyday shapes are prisms?

Activity

1 Use nets to make these prisms.

(a) Hexagonal prism.

Hexagon.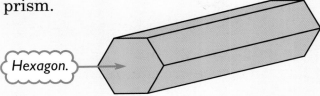

(b) Octagonal prism.

Octagon.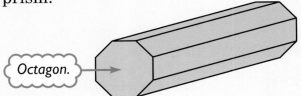

(c) L-shaped prism.

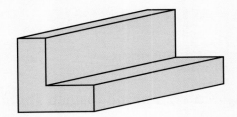

2 Copy and complete the table.

Shape	Number of faces	Number of vertices	Number of edges
Hexagonal prism			
Octagonal prism			
L-shaped prism			

 Copy and complete this rule. Faces + Vertices = Edges + ▢

This rule is called **Euler's Rule**.
Euler was a famous German mathematician of the 18th century.

 What do you notice about the hexagonal and L-shaped prisms? Explain your answer.

Finishing off

Now that you have finished this chapter you should know:

- the words **face**, **edge** and **vertex**
- that all the faces of a cube are squares
- the shape of different kinds of prism
- how to use nets to make solid shapes.

Review exercise

1 Here are the names of some solid shapes.

Cuboid		Hexagonal prism

Triangular prism   Cube   Octagonal prism

(a) Match a name to each shape below.

(i)   (ii)   (iii)   (iv)

(v)   (vi)   (vii)   (viii)

(ix)   (x)   (xi)   (xii)

(b) Which is the most common shape?

2 Michelle makes two cubes.
She glues them together, face to face.

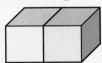

(a) What shape does she make?

She makes two more cubes and adds them to the first two.

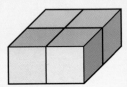

(b) What shape does she make now?

Michelle makes four more cubes.
She adds them to the first four to make a bigger cube.

(c) Where does she place the new cubes?

SU

3 Cut out the nets of a **tetrahedron** and an **octahedron**.

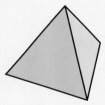

Tetrahedron

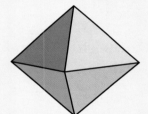

Octahedron

(a) Glue the nets to make the solids.
(b) These shapes are not prisms.
Explain why.
(c) Count the number of faces, edges and vertices for each shape.
Do these shapes obey Euler's Rule?
(d) What can you say about the faces of each shape?

Activity Design a net to make a model car.
Use squared paper.
Don't make it too complicated!
Decorate the faces of your model before you glue the edges
together.

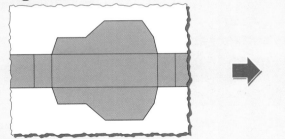

Carol sells cars.

Here are some of her sales figures.

Sales of sports cars, 2002											
Jan	Feb	Mar	Apr	May	Jun	Jul	Aug	Sep	Oct	Nov	Dec
1	0	2	3	6	6	8	7	5	3	1	6

 In which month are most sports cars sold?
In which month are fewest sports cars sold?

Task

Carol shows the sales to her manager.
She draws a **line graph**.

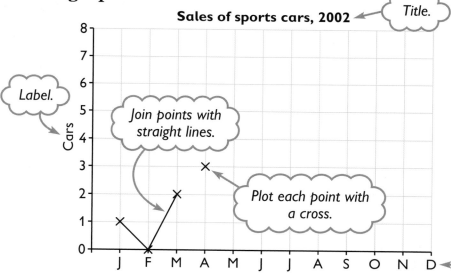

Copy and finish the graph for Carol.

 In May, sales increase by 3 cars.
  (a) Which month has the largest increase?
  (b) Which month has no change?

 The table and the graph both show data about car sales.
Which shows the information more clearly, the table or the graph?

Exercise

1

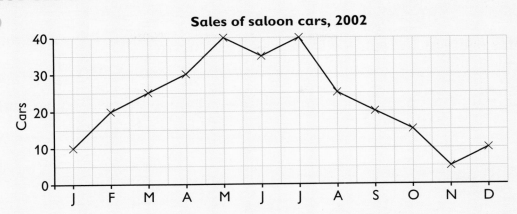

Sales of saloon cars, 2002

(a) How many saloon cars are sold in **(i)** February **(ii)** May?
(b) In which month are the fewest cars sold?
(c) In which months are the most cars sold?

su

2 A patient's body temperature is measured every hour.
Here are the recordings.

Time	Temp (°C)
8 am	37.6
9 am	37.8
10 am	37.9
11 am	37.9
12 am	38.0
1 pm	38.0
2 pm	38.0
3 pm	37.8
4 pm	37.3
5 pm	37.1
6 pm	37.0
7 pm	37.0
8 pm	37.0

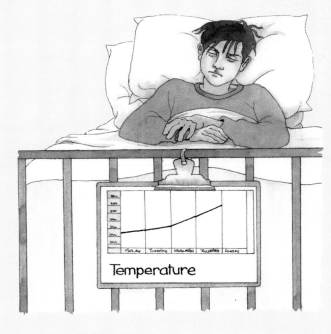

Temperature

(a) Draw a line graph to show these data.
(b) What is the highest temperature?
(c) For how long is the patient at the highest temperature?
(d) When is the temperature at 37.9 °C?

Normal body temperature is 37 °C.

(e) When does the patient reach normal temperature?
(f) When does the patient start to recover?
(g) When is the greatest temperature change?

Using graph paper

5 miles is about the same distance as 8 kilometres.

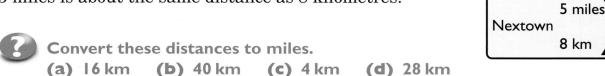

Nextown
5 miles
8 km

 Convert these distances to miles.
(a) 16 km   (b) 40 km   (c) 4 km   (d) 28 km

Task

You are going to draw a **conversion graph** between miles and kilometres.

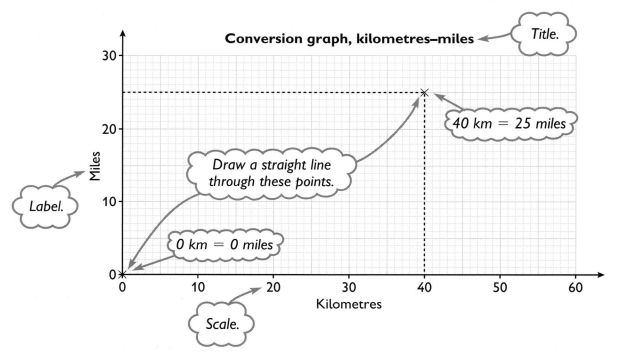

Conversion graph, kilometres–miles — Title.

Label. — Miles

Draw a straight line through these points.

0 km = 0 miles

40 km = 25 miles

Scale. — Kilometres

I Use your graph to check your answers to the questions at the top of the page.

2 Use your graph to convert these distances to kilometres.

(a) 15 miles   (b) 18 miles   (c) 21 miles   (d) 27 miles

 You can convert by calculation or by using a graph.
Which method is better?

Exercise

1 55 yards is the same distance as 50 metres.
Here is a conversion graph.

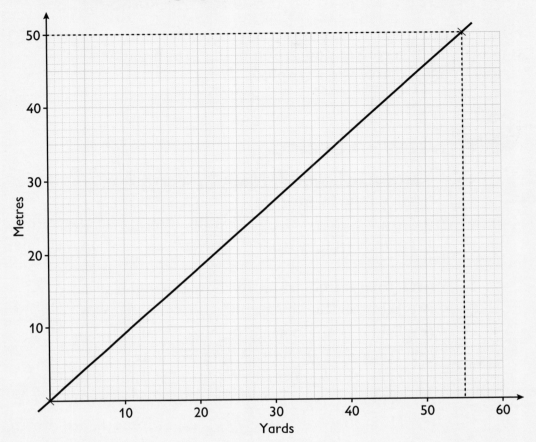

(a) Convert these distances to metres.
   (i) 20 yards   (ii) 40 yards   (iii) 15 yards   (iv) 37 yards
(b) Convert these distances to yards.
   (i) 35 metres (ii) 8 metres   (iii) 41 metres (iv) 19 metres

2 100 pints is the same amount of liquid as 57 litres.

(a) Draw a conversion graph between pints and litres.
(b) A human body contains about 5 litres of blood.
   How many pints is this?
(c) A gallon is 8 pints.
   How many litres is a gallon?
(d) Convert 30 pints into litres.

Finishing off

Now that you have finished this chapter you should know:

- how to draw and read a line graph
- how to draw a conversion graph using graph paper
- how to use a conversion graph.

Review exercise

1

Mid-day temperatures in Sheffield 1st week in August						
Sun	Mon	Tues	Weds	Thur	Fri	Sat
17 °C	18 °C	19 °C	21 °C	28 °C	29 °C	31 °C

(a) Draw a line graph to show these data.

(b) What is the lowest mid-day temperature?

(c) When is the hottest day?

(d) Tuesday is 1° hotter than Monday.
How much hotter is Wednesday than Tuesday?

(e) When is the greatest temperature change?

(f) Describe what happens to the temperature during the week.

2 £60 is the same as €90.

(a) Draw a conversion graph between pounds and euros.

(b) A hire car costs €70 for one day.
How much is the price in pounds?

(c) Andre buys a meal for £25.
How much does this cost in euros?

(d) Mercy buys a present for €53.
Convert the price into pounds.

Trainers £60 €90

3

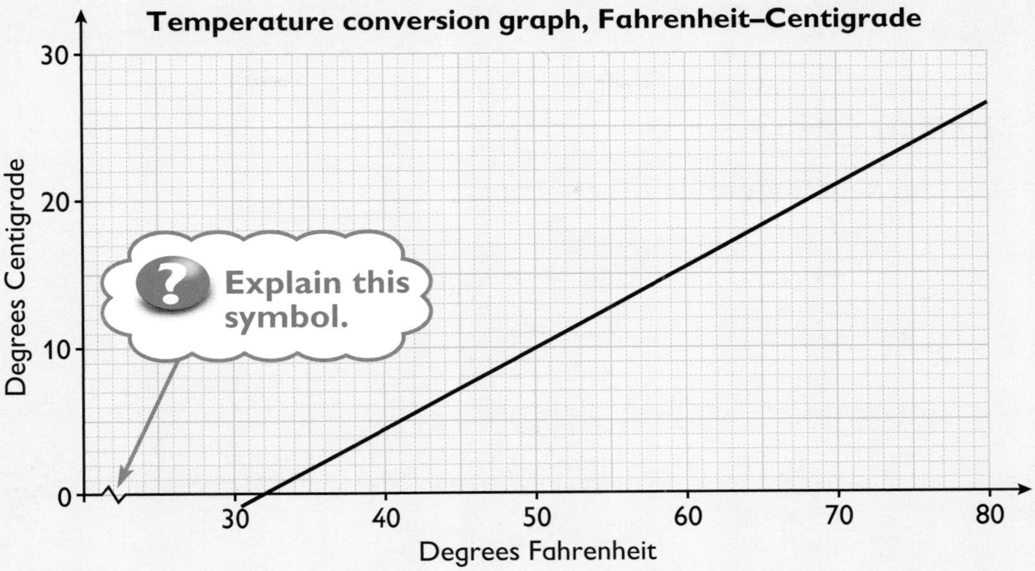

Temperature conversion graph, Fahrenheit–Centigrade

? Explain this symbol.

(a) Comfortable room temperature is 20 °C.
Convert this to Fahrenheit.

(b) Water freezes at 0 °C.
What is the freezing point in degrees Fahrenheit?

(c) On a sunny day the temperature is 76 °F.
What is this in Centigrade?

(d) What is 45 °F in Centigrade?

4

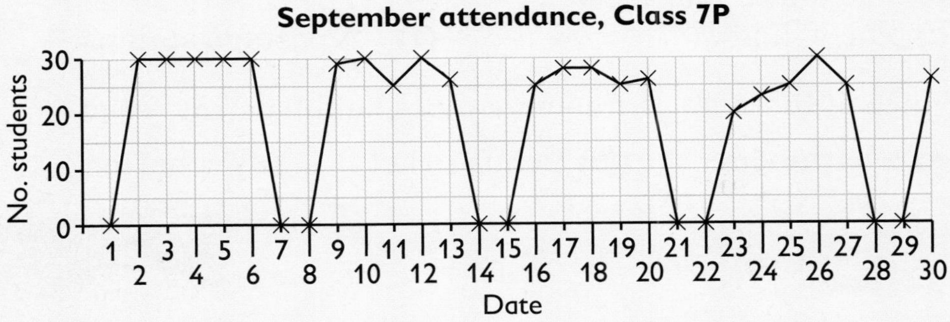

September attendance, Class 7P

This graph shows the attendance of Class 7P during September.

(a) How many students attend on 2nd September?
(b) What is the least attendance?
(c) What day of the week is 7th September?
(d) How many students do you think there are in the class?

Perimeter

This is the sports field at Ali's school.

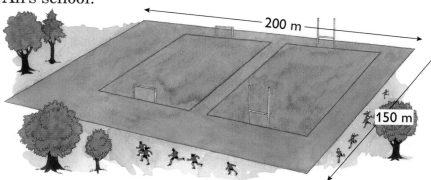

Before a football match, the team run all the way round the field to warm up.

 How far do the players run?

> The distance round the outside of a shape is called the **perimeter**.

Task

I Measure the perimeter of each of these items.

(a) The cover of this book.   **(b)** The door.
(c) The top of your desk.   **(d)** The classroom floor.
(e) The window.   **(f)** A postage stamp.

2 Which of these measurements could be the perimeter of

(a) a bathroom   **(b)** a bus ticket   **(c)** a button?

| 15 metres | 30 millimetres | 20 centimetres |

 What is the perimeter of this shape?

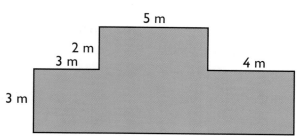

5 m

2 m
3 m

4 m

3 m

Exercise

1 **(i)** Name these shapes.
(ii) Measure the sides of each shape.
(iii) Work out the perimeter of each shape.

(a)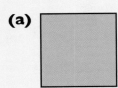

(b)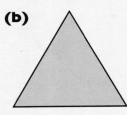

(d)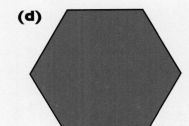

(c)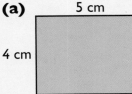

2 Work out the perimeters of these shapes (do not measure the sides).

(a) 5 cm

4 cm

(b) 3 cm

3 Work out the perimeter of this field.

80 m

50 m

80 m

20 m

Activity On centimetre squared paper, draw as many different rectangles as you can, each with a perimeter of 24 cm.

Area

Alan

> Which photograph takes up more space?

Christina

Christina draws round the photographs on **squared paper**.
Here are their shapes.

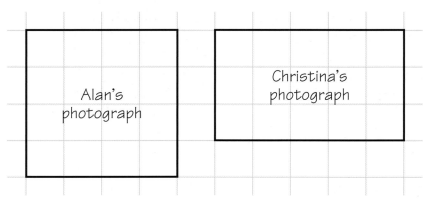

Alan's photograph

Christina's photograph

> Each square on the paper represents 1 square centimetre or 1 cm².

The area of Christina's photograph is 15 cm².

 What is the area of Alan's photograph?

Area is an amount of flat surface.

Task

Look at the cat.

1 How many **whole** squares are there in this shape?

2 How many **half** squares are there?

Each square represents 1 cm².

3 What is the total area of the shape?

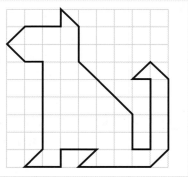

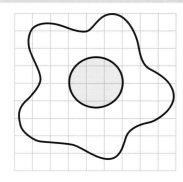

 What is the area of this fried egg?
(Each square represents 1 cm².)
How do you find it?

 Is this an accurate answer or an estimate?

Exercise

1 What is the area of each of these shapes?
(Each square represents 1 cm².)

(a) 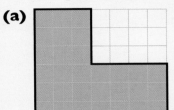 (b) 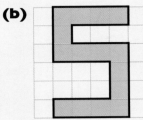 (c)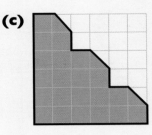

2 (a) On centimetre squared paper, draw round your foot.
(b) Find an **estimate** for the area of your foot.

3 Look at this shape. Each square represents 1 cm².

(a) What is the area of the rectangle?
(b) What is the area of the shaded triangle?
(c) What do you notice?

4 The area of this shaded triangle is 5 cm².

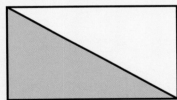

What is the area of the rectangle?

Activity **1** On squared paper, draw as many different rectangles as you
can, each with an area of 24 squares.

2 Which rectangle has the largest perimeter?

3 Which has the smallest perimeter?

4 What do you notice?

Volume

Samir

 What shape is the box?

Each sugar cube is 1 cm long, 1 cm high and 1 cm wide.
Its **volume** is 1 cubic centimetre.

Volume is an amount of space.

Write 1 cubic centimetre as 1 cm³ or 1 cc.

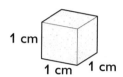

1 cm
1 cm   1 cm

Task

1 How many sugar cubes fit in one layer in the box above?

2 How many layers are there in the box?

3 How many cubes are there altogether?

4 What is the volume of the box?

5 **(a)** What is the volume of this box?
   (b) What do you notice?

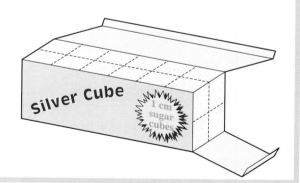

6 Design a box to hold 60 sugar cubes.

Look at these tins and bottles.

The volume of a container is also called its capacity.

 How much liquid does each one hold?

 What units are used for liquids?

330 ml

Red Wine
75 cl

Lemonade
2 litres

Exercise

1 John has made these shapes with some building bricks.
Each brick is 1 cm³.
What is the volume of each shape?

(a)

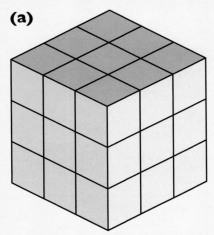

(b)

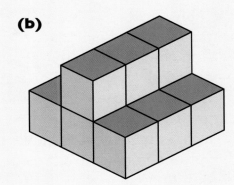

(c)

2 Which of these units would you use to describe

(a) the volume of a room
(b) the amount of wine in a bottle
(c) the amount of water in a bath
(d) the volume of your pencil case?

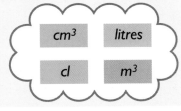

cm³   litres

cl   m³

Activity   Collect information about the engine sizes of different cars.

How are all the engine sizes given? What does this mean?

Make a poster showing pictures of your favourite cars and giving their engine sizes.

Finishing off

Now that you have finished this chapter you should:

- be able to
  - measure and calculate the perimeter of a flat shape
  - find the area of a flat shape by counting squares
  - estimate the area of an irregular shape by counting squares
  - find the volume of a shape by counting cubes
- know that
  - area is measured in square units, for example cm^2
  - volume is measured in cubic units, for example cm^3
  - liquid is measured in litres.

Review exercise

1 Kim draws a plan of the patio in her garden.

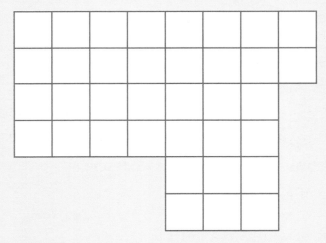

Each slab is a square, 1 metre long.

(a) What is the area of the patio?

Kim puts a new fence all round the patio.

(b) How long is the fence?

2 This box holds 36 sugar cubes.

(a) How many layers of sugar cubes are there?

Another box holds 24 sugar cubes.
There are 3 layers of sugar cubes in the box.

(b) How many sugar cubes are there in one layer?

Activity

You have 4 square tiles.
The tiles can only be put together edge to edge, like this.

1 On squared paper draw **all** the possible arrangements of 4 tiles.

2 What is the area of each arrangement of tiles? What do you notice?

3 Find the perimeter of each arrangement.
What do you notice?

Investigation

Mrs Green is building a new rectangular patio for her garden.

She has 18 square slabs. Each slab measures 1 metre by 1 metre.
She wants to have a flower bed in the middle of the patio and she must use
all the slabs.

One design would look like this.

On squared paper, draw as many possible designs
as you can for Mrs Green's patio.

Michelle — I have been working really hard.

What about the rest of you?

Mrs Shah — Yes.

Samir

Class 7G have another Reward lesson.

Back to back drawing

Michelle and Samir play **Back to back drawing**.

Samir starts with a blank grid.

Michelle has a picture.

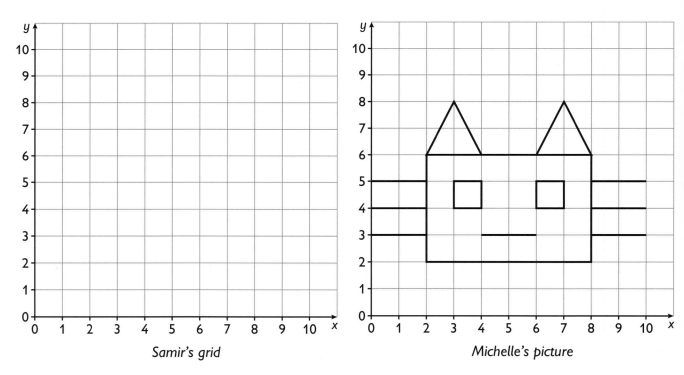

Samir's grid

Michelle's picture

They sit back to back.

Draw a rectangle.
Start at (2, 2). Go to
(8, 2), then (8, 6).

Not so fast!

? **At the end Samir's drawing looks like this.**
What has gone wrong?

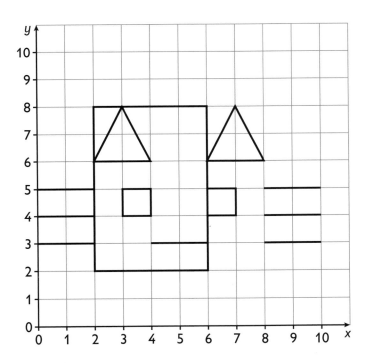

Task

Play **Back to back drawing** with a friend.
Take it in turns to make up a picture and give the instructions.

Give your pictures to other pairs.

Decision tree diagrams

Anju

Rajah

Gita

Khan

Natani

? How do you tell these big cats apart?

Task

This is a **decision tree diagram**. Work through it with each big cat. Say what type of cat each of them is.

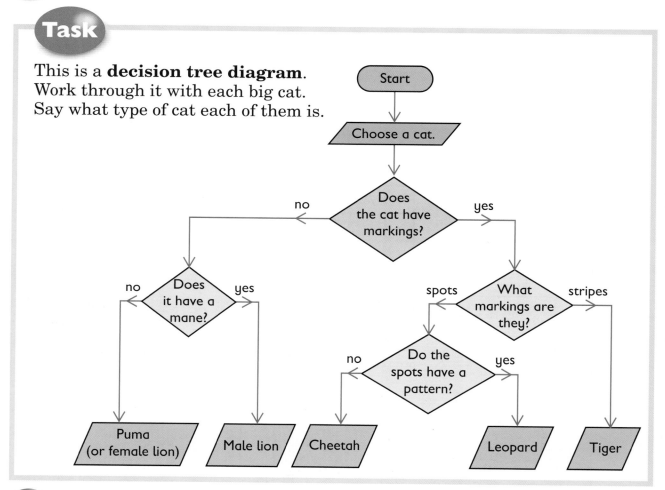

Start

Choose a cat.

Does the cat have markings? — no / yes

Does it have a mane? — no / yes

What markings are they? — spots / stripes

Do the spots have a pattern? — no / yes

Puma (or female lion)

Male lion

Cheetah

Leopard

Tiger

? The RSPCA wants to find homes for some cats. How do they describe each cat?

(a)

Bagpuss

(b)

Whiskers

(c)

Custard

(d)

Tabatha

(e)

Felix

Exercise

1 Use the tree diagram to sort these triangles.

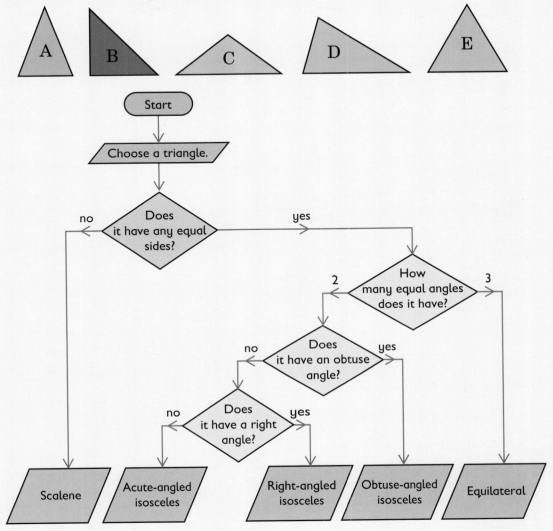

2 You want to sort these quadrilaterals.
What questions do you need to ask?

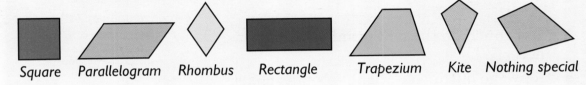

Square   Parallelogram   Rhombus   Rectangle   Trapezium   Kite   Nothing special

Activity Design a tree diagram to sort these dogs.

Alsatian   St Bernard   Retriever   Bulldog   Spaniel

Flow charts

Michelle designs a flow chart.

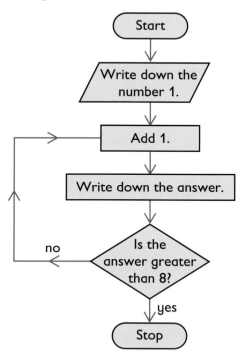

Michelle

Use Michelle's flow chart to complete the table.

 What do you notice about the numbers written down?

Number written down	Is the number greater than 8?
1	No
2	No
9	Yes

Task

Harry is going to change Michelle's flow chart to make the odd numbers from 1 to 9. Can you help him?

1 Write down the odd numbers from 1 to 9.

2 How much do the odd numbers increase by?

3 Copy the outline of Michelle's flow chart. Fill it in so that it gives the odd numbers. You only have to change the third box.

4 Now rewrite Michelle's flow chart to give the even numbers from 2 to 20.

I only need to change one box in Michelle's flow chart.

Harry

? **You want the 5 times table.**
How do you change Michelle's flow chart?

Exercise

SU

1 Meena designs a flow chart.
She tries to make the 3 times table.

(a) Write down the numbers made
by her flow chart. Use the table.

Meena

> Whoops!
> This is not the 3 times
> table. I have done
> something wrong!

Number written down	Is the number greater than 20?
1	No
4	No
22	Yes

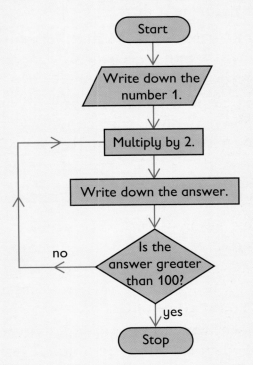

(b) She needs to change the second box. Draw the new box out for her.

2 (a) Write down the numbers
made by this flow chart.

(b) Change one box in the flow chart to give these numbers.

    1   5   25   125

Number sequences

John writes down a number sequence.
He starts with the number 1 and adds 5.

1   6   11   16   21   26   31   36

? **What patterns do you notice in his numbers?**
What are the next 2 terms in the sequence?

*The 'gap' between the numbers is called the **difference**.*

John

Task

Mercy thinks of another number pattern.

1 Write down the first 10 terms in Mercy's sequence.

2 (a) How is it like John's sequence?
   (b) How is it different?

3 (a) Write down the number sequence that starts at 5 and increases by 5.
   (b) What types of number does this give you?

4 (a) Start with different numbers and add 5 each time. Write down the sequences.
   (b) Write down the patterns you notice.

I will start with 2 then add 5.

Mercy

Humza writes down the first 2 numbers in a sequence.

2   4   __   __   __   __   __

? **Continue the sequence for him.**
How many different sequences can you find?

Exercise

1 Find the next two numbers in these sequences.

(a) 2   4   6   8

(b) 7   11   15   19

(c) 20   17   14   11

(d) 20   15   10   5

(e) 1   2   4   8

(f) 1   4   9   16

(g) 1   3   6   10

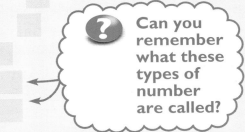

Can you remember what these types of number are called?

2 For each of these sequences, find the differences between the terms.

(a) 6   13   20   27   34

(b) 100   105   110   115   120

(c) 2   3   5   8   12

(d) 10   8   6   4   2

3 Write down the missing numbers in these sequences.

(a) 6   9   18   21

(b) 0   16   24   40

(c) 23   19   11   3

(d) 1   11

(e) 5   7   10   25

Activity

SU Look at this sequence. You add 4, each time.

0 4 8 12 16 20 24 28 32 36

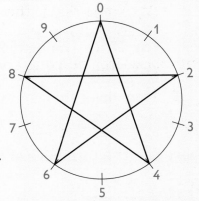

The last digits of these numbers are coloured in red.
These numbers are joined in order in the circle.
Make your own patterns using the following sequences.

1 Add 2 sequence: 0 2 4 6 8 10.

2 Add 3 sequence: 0 3 6 9 12 15 18 21 24 27 30.

3 Add 5 sequence.

4 Add 6 sequence.

5 Your own 'add' sequence.

Patterns of growth

Karl forms a pattern with matchsticks.

? **What does the next diagram look like?
How many matchsticks are there
in the 10th diagram?**

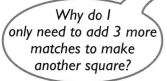

*Why do I
only need to add 3 more
matches to make
another square?*

Karl

Task

I Copy and fill in the table for Karl's matchstick pattern.

Number of squares	1	2	3	4	5	10
Number of matchsticks	4					

2 What pattern do you see in the number of matchsticks.

3 Why does this happen?

4 Karl now makes his pattern vertically like this.

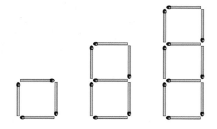

    (a) Draw the next 2 diagrams.

    (b) Make a table. Put in the results for the number of matchsticks.

5 How does this compare to Karl's first pattern? Why?

Here are the numbers of matchsticks for another pattern.

5   9   13   17   21   25

? **Draw some matchstick pictures for this pattern.**

Exercise

For each matchstick pattern:

(a) draw the next two matchstick patterns

(b) copy and complete the table for the first 6 patterns

(c) predict the next two answers in the table

(d) describe the patterns in the answers.

1

   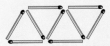

Number of triangles	1	2	3	4	5	6	7	8
Number of matchsticks	3							

2

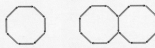 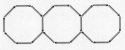 

Number of hexagons	1	2	3	4	5	6	7	8
Number of matchsticks	6							

3

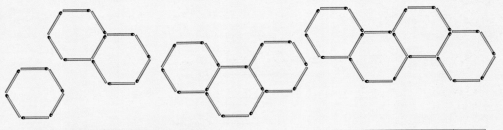

Number of octagons	1	2	3	4	5	6	7	8
Number of matchsticks	8							

Activity   Design your own pattern using matchsticks.

(a) Draw the first 6 diagrams.

(b) Make a table to show the results.

(c) Comment on the patterns in the numbers.

(d) Explain these patterns.

Finishing off

Review exercise

1 This is a never ending flow chart.

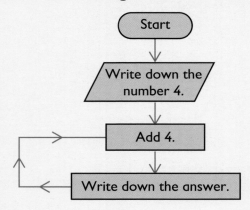

(a) Write down the first 10 numbers generated by the chart.

(b) What types of numbers are these?

(c) What are the differences between these numbers?

(d) What are the next 2 numbers in the pattern?

(e) What is the 20th number?

(f) What is the 100th number?

The number 70 can be generated by the flow chart.

Jo

(g) Explain why Jo is wrong.

(h) What numbers between 70 and 80 can be generated by the flow chart?

2 Look at these matchstick patterns.

(a) Draw the next diagram.

(b) Copy and fill in the table of results.

Length of arm	1	2	3	4	5
Number of matchsticks	4				

(c) What do you notice about the pattern in the number of matchsticks?

(d) Why does the number of matchsticks increase in this way?

3 Use the tree diagram to sort the numbers from 1 to 20.
Put the numbers in two groups. Use circles like the ones below.

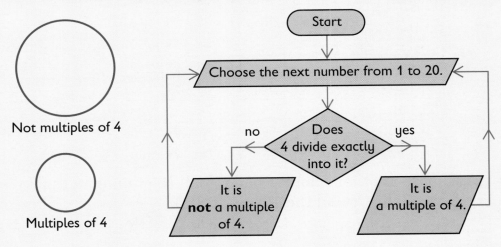

Investigation Investigate the perimeters of these squares.

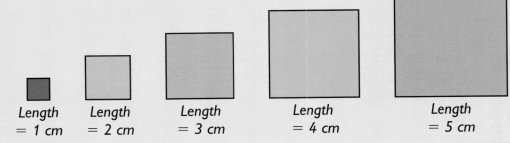

23 Accuracy

Rounding numbers

I think there were about 29 people at the disco last night.

Humza

I think there were 32.

Megan

So to the nearest 10 there were 30.

Mrs Shah

? **What other numbers round to 30 when given to the nearest 10?**

Task

1 (a) Copy the '100 square' below.
The numbers that round to 10 are all shaded in 1 colour.

1	2	3	4	5	6	7	8	9	10
11	12	13	14	15	16	17	18	19	20
21	22	23	24	25	26	27	28	29	30
31	32	33	34	35	36	37	38	39	40
41	42	43	44	45	46	47	48	49	50
51	52	53	54	55	56	57	58	59	60
61	62	63	64	65	66	67	68	69	70
71	72	73	74	75	76	77	78	79	80
81	82	83	84	85	86	87	88	89	90
91	92	93	94	95	96	97	98	99	100

(b) Choose another colour. Shade in all the numbers that round to 20.
(c) Repeat this for all the 10s up to 100.

2 Copy this number line.
Circle the whole numbers that round to 160 to the nearest 10.

151 152 153 154 155 156 157 158 159 160 161 162 163 164 165 166 167 168 169

? **Complete this sentence.**
At Mark's school the number of students
is between ⬚ **and** ⬚ **.**

To the nearest 100, there are 800 people at my school.

Mark

? **What numbers round to 4000 to the nearest 1000?**

Exercise

1 Round these numbers to the nearest 10.

(a) 31 **(b)** 48 **(c)** 56 **(d)** 82 **(e)** 25 **(f)** 98 **(g)** 164
(h) 201 **(i)** 195 **(j)** 649 **(k)** 5 **(l)** 399 **(m)** 2 **(n)** 855

2 Round these numbers to the nearest 100.

(a) 345 **(b)** 408 **(c)** 633 **(d)** 755 **(e)** 50 **(f)** 849
(g) 234 **(h)** 1098 **(i)** 78 **(j)** 3499 **(k)** 5067 **(l)** 4610

3 Copy the table and fill in the missing numbers.

	Nearest 1000	Nearest 100	Nearest 10
1762			1760
1215			
2649	3000		
9053			
4895		4900	
7382			

4 Draw number lines showing which whole numbers round to

(a) 290, to the nearest 10 **(b)** 400, to the nearest 100.

5 Big numbers in newspapers are often rounded.
Write each headline again using a rounded number.

Sports Daily

5879 at local football match

Evening News

Mum wins **£7226** *in lottery*

Local Lottery
THE ESTIMATED JACKPOT FOR
SAT 14 OCT 2005 IS £5M

Local Echo

Man walks 1783 miles for charity

Activity Change the order of the digits **3**, **7** and **9** to make six different
3-digit numbers.

For example, 379 or 793 .

Use your numbers to make a table like the one below.

Number	Nearest 100	Nearest 10
379	400	380
793	800	790

Repeat this activity using the digits **8**, **1** and **5**.

Rounding to the nearest whole number

Sophie and Jack are measuring leaves.

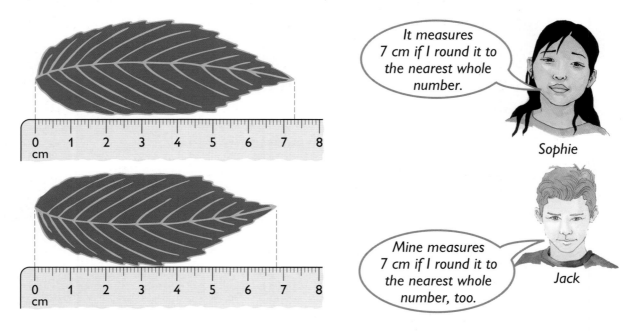

It measures 7 cm if I round it to the nearest whole number.

Sophie

Mine measures 7 cm if I round it to the nearest whole number, too.

Jack

? **What is the smallest measurement on your ruler that can be rounded to 7 cm? What is the largest?**

? **What measurements on your ruler can be rounded to**
   (a) 14 cm   **(b)** 20 cm?

Task

Decimal bingo: a class game

1 Draw a 3 × 3 square like the one on the right.
   Write a **different** whole number between 1 and 20 in each square.

2 Choose someone to be the caller.
   He or she calls out a series of decimal numbers, like 8.9 or 16.2.

3 Round each number to the nearest whole number.
   If the number is in your square, cross it out.

4 The first person to get a line of 3 crosses wins (shout 'Bingo!').

? **What is 17.34 rounded to the nearest whole number?**
   What about 25.861?

Exercise

1 Round these to the nearest whole number.

(a) 6.3 (b) 4.8 (c) 8.1 (d) 12.9 (e) 48.5 (f) 17.2
(g) 55.2 (h) 39.8 (i) 106.7 (j) 413.3 (k) 399.6 (l) 79.7

2 Round these amounts to the nearest pound (£).

(a) £3.19 (b) £14.58 (c) £26.02 (d) £2.50
(e) £19.67 (f) £207.81 (g) £199.82 (h) £619.01

3 Write each measurement to the nearest centimetre.

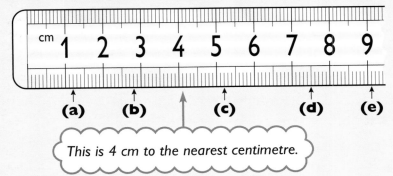

This is 4 cm to the nearest centimetre.

4

My pencil is exactly 12 cm. — Christina

My pencil is 12 cm to the nearest centimetre. My pencil is shorter than Christina's. — Harry

My pencil is 12 cm to the nearest centimetre. My pencil is longer than Christina's. — Mercy

For each of these statements, answer 'May be true' or 'Definitely false'.

(a) Harry's pencil is 11.7 cm. (b) Mercy's pencil is 12.5 cm.
(c) Harry's pencil is 11.5 cm. (d) Mercy's pencil is 12.3 cm.

Activity Choose some whole numbers.
Make a poster showing some decimal numbers that can be rounded to each of your whole numbers.

Sensible answers

Tim and his friends go to Burger Delight.

	Pizza	£3.99		Fries	89p
	Cheeseburger	£1.99		Donut	£1.09
	Burger meal	£2.99		Ice cream	99p
	Chickenburger	£1.49		All drinks	95p

? **Michelle buys 3 burger meals. Roughly how much does she pay?**

I ice cream costs 99p, that's about £1. We want 4 ice creams, so we'll pay about £4.

Tim

? **John buys 1 drink and 2 burger meals. Roughly how much does he pay?**

Task

1 Roughly how much does each of these orders cost?

(a) 2 pizzas

(b) 4 burger meals

(c) 1 pizza / 2 ice creams

(d) 3 cheeseburgers / 1 pizza

(e) 1 chickenburger / 2 fries

(f) 1 donut / 1 drink

(g) 2 fries / 1 drink

(h) 2 chickenburgers / 1 drink / 1 donut

2 You have £10 to spend.
Choose a meal for yourself and a friend at Burger Delight.

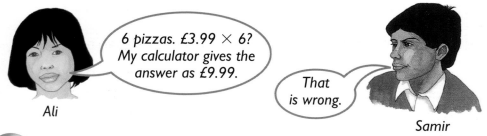

6 pizzas. £3.99 × 6? My calculator gives the answer as £9.99.

Ali

That is wrong.

Samir

? **How does Samir know that Ali is wrong?**

Exercise

1 Find the rough cost of

(a) 5 bars of chocolate at 99p each

(b) 2 magazines at £1.95 each

(c) 4 books at £3.99 each

(d) 3 CDs at £9.99 each.

2 Copy and complete this table. The first one is done for you.

Sum	Rough calculation	Rough answer
19 + 38	20 + 40	60
42 + 61		
71 − 27		
199 − 13		
148 + 58		
41 ÷ 9		
19 × 11		

3 For each of these sums, choose the most sensible **rough** answer.

(a) 78 + 19   Answers: **(i)** 90   **(ii)** 100   **(iii)** 110

(b) 61 − 29   Answers: **(i)** 30   **(ii)** 40   **(iii)** 50

(c) 147 + 31   Answers: **(i)** 160   **(ii)** 170   **(iii)** 180

4 Copy and complete these sentences.

(a) 46 hours is about _____ days.

(b) 27 minutes is about _____ an hour.

(c) 203 centimetres is about _____ metres.

(d) 98 millimetres is about _____ centimetres.

(e) 614 pence is about _____ pounds.

Activity

1 Make up 10 sums, 5 that are right and 5 that are **obviously** wrong.

For example   54 + 68 = 122   ✓ RIGHT

                    78 − 51 = 129   ✗ WRONG   (as 80 − 50 = 30)

2 Swap your sums with a friend.
Can he or she spot the wrong answers?

Finishing off

Now that you have finished this chapter you should be able to:

- round a number to the nearest 1, 10, 100 and 1000
- make a sensible rough estimate of an answer.

Review exercise

1 Round these amounts to the nearest 10p.

(a) 42p   (b) 67p   (c) 8p   (d) 96p
(e) 55p   (f) 123p   (g) 479p

2 Copy this table and round these numbers.

	Nearest 100	Nearest 10
371		
402		
6399		
1045		

3 Round the measurements to the nearest 10 mm.

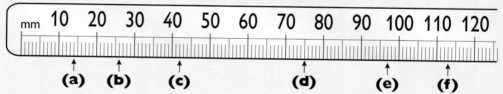

4 This table shows the number of kilometres between some cities.

	London	Birmingham	Cardiff
Birmingham	175		
Cardiff	244	163	
Glasgow	629	459	592

(a) How far is it from Cardiff to Birmingham to the nearest 10 kilometres?
(b) How far is it from Glasgow to London to the nearest 10 kilometres?
(c) How far is it from Glasgow to Cardiff to the nearest 100 kilometres?

5 Round these amounts to the nearest pound (£).

(a) £2.41   (b) £7.16   (c) £3.01   (d) £5.50   (e) £4.22
(f) £8.49   (g) £9.74   (h) £15.30   (i) £27.65   (j) £49.79

6 Round these amounts to the nearest 10p.

(a) £1.43 (b) £6.57 (c) £3.28 (d) £12.41 (e) £8.65 (f) £26.14

7 Here are the speeds of some animals.
Round each one to the nearest whole number.

(a) Sailfish 108.8 km per hour
(b) Fastest racehorse 69.6 km per hour
(c) Greyhound 67.1 km per hour
(d) Centipede 1.8 km per hour

8 Round each weight to the nearest kilogram.

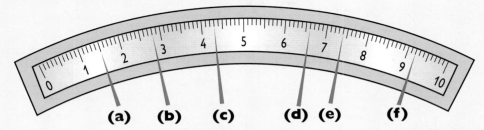

9 Copy and complete this table. The first one is done for you.

Sum	Rough calculation	Rough answer	Accurate answer
31 + 49	30 + 50	80	80
29 + 44			
65 − 49			
23 + 37			
62 − 48			

10 Work out these. Round your answer to the nearest whole number.

(a) 12 ÷ 5   (b) 25 ÷ 3   (c) 79 ÷ 5
(d) 27 ÷ 10 (e) 59 ÷ 2   (f) 155 ÷ 50

Activity The United Kingdom's tallest mountain is Ben Nevis.
It is 1343 metres high.

Find the height of 6 more mountains. Round each height to the
nearest 100 m.
Make a table like this one to show your results.

Mountain	Exact number	Rounded number
Ben Nevis	1343 m	1300 m

Probability scales

I am unlikely to go to the moon.

It is likely that my bus will be late.

It is certain that Christmas will be on 25th December.

Look at the words on this probability scale.

Impossible	Unlikely		Likely	Certain
0		$\frac{1}{2}$		1

Something that is **impossible** has a probability of 0.

The probability that a coin will land 'heads' is $\frac{1}{2}$.

Something that is **certain** has a probability of 1.

? **Say something that is impossible. What about certain?**

? **50–50 chance and evens mean the same.**
Which number on the scale also means evens?

Task

Make a class poster.

1 Copy the probability scale above.

2 Add the terms **very unlikely**, **very likely** and **evens** to your scale.

3 Write the following phrases in the correct place on your scale.

It will rain tomorrow.	I will score 7 when I throw a die.

It will snow on Christmas day.	Easter Day will be on a Sunday.

4 Think of some more statements.

5 Add these to your probability scale.

? **Can you have a probability bigger than 1?**

Exercise

1 Match the statements below with the words **certain**, **very likely**, **likely**, **evens**, **unlikely**, **very unlikely** and **impossible**.

(a) A coin will land tails.
(b) There is a monster in Loch Ness.
(c) The sun will rise tomorrow.
(d) I will throw a five or a six when I throw a die.
(e) You will live to be 199 years old.
(f) Someone will win the lottery jackpot this weekend.
(g) You will live to be 60 years old.

2 The probability that a coin will land heads is $\frac{1}{2}$ (evens).
Copy this table and write each event in the correct place.

Probability		
Smaller than $\frac{1}{2}$	$\frac{1}{2}$	**Bigger than $\frac{1}{2}$**
	A coin will land heads	

(a) It will rain tomorrow.
(b) Your team will win their next match.
(c) You will eat chips this week.
(d) The world record for the marathon will be broken.
(e) This spinner will land on red.
(f) The temperature in August will reach 20 °C.

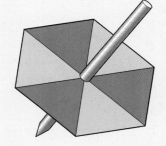

3 Look at this probability scale for the weather on July 1st 2020 in London.

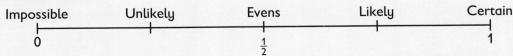

(a) Copy the scale and add the following in the correct places.

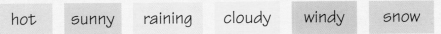

   hot   sunny   raining   cloudy   windy   snow

(b) Draw another scale for the weather in Spain on the same day.

Probability

The probability that this die lands on a 6 is $\frac{1}{6}$.

Ali

? **What is the probability that the die lands on a 4?**

? **What is the probability that the die lands on an even number?**

Task

1 Throw a die 60 times.
Record the result of each throw on a copy of this frequency chart.

? **What does frequency mean?**

Number on die	Tally	Frequency
1		
2		
3		
4		
5		
6		

2 Compare your results with a friend.

? **What do you notice?**

3 **(a)** Put all the results from your class together.
(b) How many times do you expect to throw a 6?
(c) How many 6s have the class thrown?

? **Why is the frequency about the same for each number?**

? **What is the probability that this spinner will land on win?**

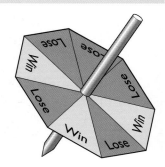

Exercise

1 There is a prize behind one of the doors.
Tim chooses door B.
What is the probability that he wins
the prize?

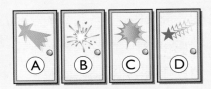

2 What is the probability
that a black fish eats
the worm?

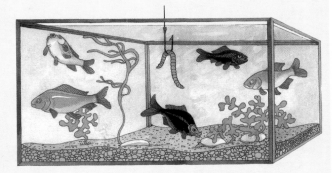

3 Karl chooses one of these cards
without looking.

(a) What is the probability that
he chooses the 7?

(b) What is the probability that
he chooses an even number?

4

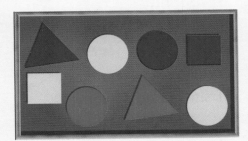

Meena chooses a shape from this box.
What is the probability that the shape she chooses is
(a) a circle   **(b)** red   **(c)** a yellow circle?

Activity   Work with a friend.
You will need a bag, 3 red balls and 2 green balls.
Put the balls in the bag.
Ask your friend to take a ball from the bag, write down the
colour and then put the ball back in the bag.
Your friend should do this 25 times.

? How many times do you expect your friend to choose a
green ball?

? Do your results agree with this?

Finishing off

Now that you have finished this chapter you should:

- know how to use words like **certain**, **unlikely**, **likely** and **impossible** when describing probability
- know what is meant by evens or a probability of $\frac{1}{2}$
- be able to calculate simple probabilities.

Review exercise

1 Match the events below with the words **certain**, **likely**, **evens**, **unlikely** and **impossible**.

(a) You will come to school tomorrow.
(b) You will grow to 2 metres tall.
(c) A coin will land heads.
(d) The sun will rise tomorrow.
(e) The next car to pass will be a red mini.
(f) It will snow this winter.

2 The following names are put in a hat.

| Mary | Malcolm | Michael | Martha | Mervin | Miriam | Melanie |

A name is pulled out.
What is the probability that the name chosen

(a) is Malcolm
(b) is a girl's name
(c) is a boy's name
(d) begins with M
(e) begins with D
(f) ends with M?

3

Christmas Raffle
Any ticket ending in 0 wins a prize!

100 tickets are sold. They are numbered 1 to 100.

(a) How many winning tickets are there?
(b) Jane buys a ticket. What is the probability she wins a prize?

4 What is the probability that the spinner will land on

(a) an orange
(b) a fruit (orange or lemon)
(c) a bell?

Activity

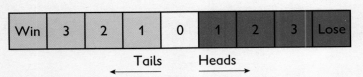

| Win | 3 | 2 | 1 | 0 | 1 | 2 | 3 | Lose |

Tails ← → Heads

1 Place a counter on the 0 on this grid.

2 Throw a coin.

Tails

Move 1 place left.

Heads

Move 1 place right.

3 Play the game until you win or lose.

4 How many people in your class win?

5 How many lose?

6 What do you think about the probability of winning?
Is it likely, unlikely or evens?

Activity

You need 2 coins. Throw both coins.
The chart shows how you can win and how you can lose.

Win	Lose
Head, head	Head, tail
Tail, tail	Tail, head

1 What do you think about the probability of winning this game?
Is it likely, unlikely or evens?

2 Play the game 20 times.
Write down the number of times you win and the number of times you lose.

3 Do you still agree with your answer in **1**?

Combining operations

What is
1 + 2 × 3?

9

Pete

7

Kim

? How did Pete get his answer? What about Kim?
Who is right?

? + and × are called operations.
What other operations do you know?

Task

Meena is planning her birthday. She will be 12.

Mum,
what shall I
do?

Invite
some friends.
You can spend
£100.

Meena

Meena decides to go to Film World.
Help Meena plan her party.

Think about

(a) how many people she can invite
(b) what they will eat.

FILM WORLD
PRICES

Film	£4.50	Ice cream	£2.00
Popcorn	£4.00	Chips	£2.50
Drinks	£6.00	Hot dog	£3.00
Pizza	£6.00	Burger	£4.00

? Work out these.
(a) 35 ÷ 5 − 3   **(b)** 3 × 7 + 2 × 6

? Which operations did you use in each?
In what order are they used? Is the order important?

Exercise

1 Work out these.

(a) $4 \times 6 + 5$ **(b)** $3 \times 7 - 9$ **(c)** $6 + 3 \times 5$ **(d)** $10 - 2 \times 5$

2 Work out these.

(a) $8 + 20 \div 4$ **(b)** $16 - 15 \div 3$ **(c)** $25 - 15 \div 5$ **(d)** $32 \div 4 - 2$

3 Work out these.

(a) $3 \times 2 + 5 \times 6$ **(b)** $9 \times 2 + 7 \times 4$

(c) $\dfrac{5 + 7 + 6 + 2}{4}$ **(d)** $\dfrac{3 + 7 + 6 + 5 + 14}{5}$

4 Find the batting average for each of these cricketers.

(a) Sahil	35	45	8	65	82
(b) Ben	25	20	14	12	4
(c) Chris	17	51	2	0	0

5 It's holiday time and Mercy and her friends are changing their spending money into euros.

> To change pounds (£) to euros (€):
> 1 Divide the £s by 2
> 2 Multiply the answer by 3.

Work out how much spending money each has in euros.

(a) Mercy £150
(b) Karl £80
(c) Christina £120
(d) Harry £68

6
> To change °Fahrenheit to °Celsius:
> 1 Subtract 32
> 2 Divide the answer by 9
> 3 Multiply that answer by 5.

Change these temperatures into Celsius.

(a) $50\,°\text{F}$ **(b)** $77\,°\text{F}$ **(c)** $212\,°\text{F}$ **(d)** $32\,°\text{F}$

Brackets

I'll have 3 please.

Jack

Jack works out 3×17.

3 lots of 10 = 30   and   3 lots of 7 = 21
so 3 lots of 17 = 30 + 21 = 51

? **Explain how this works.**

Task

Copy and complete this table for the shop.

Apples	1	2	3	4	5	6	7	8	9	10
Cost	17p		51p			£1.02				

You are really using brackets.

Jack's mum writes:

3×17
$3 \times (10 + 7)$
$3 \times 10 + 3 \times 7$
$30 + 21$
51

? **Work out $(20 + 6) \times 4$. What is 26×4?**

? **How can you work out** **(a)** 5×17 **(b)** 5×37?

? **How can you work out** **(a)** 3×97 **(b)** 5×483?

Exercise

1 Work out these.

(a) (i) 3×5 (ii) 3×50 (b) (i) 6×4 (ii) 6×40

(c) (i) 5×8 (ii) 50×8 (d) (i) 7×7 (ii) 70×7

(e) (i) 3×2 (ii) 30×2 (f) (i) 9×5 (ii) 90×5

(g) (i) 6×3 (ii) 60×3 (h) (i) 4×7 (ii) 40×7

2 (a) Work out these.

(i) 5×30 (ii) 5×7

> $30 + 7 = 37$

(b) Use your answers to part (a) to work out 5×37.

3 Work out these.

(a) (i) 40×3 (ii) 7×3

(b) What is 47×3?

4 Work out these.

(a) (i) 20×6 (ii) 8×6

(b) What is 28×6?

5 Work out these.

(a) (i) 5×70 (ii) 5×2

(b) What is 5×72?

6 Work out these.

(a) 100×4 (b) 2×4 (c) 102×4 (d) 98×4

7 Work out these.

(a) 101×7 (b) 99×7 (c) 1001×7 (d) 999×7

8 Look at the diagram.

(a) Find area A.

(b) Find area B.

(c) Find the total area.

(d) What is 17×5?

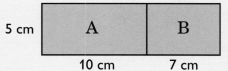

5 cm   A   B

10 cm   7 cm

More division

A group of 20 people hire a submarine.
They share the cost equally.

Undersea Trips
Neptune submarine
£480 group rate
Max 20 people

John

We need
to work out
480 ÷ 20.

I don't
know my 20
times table.

Michelle

? **Look at Michelle's working out.
What has she done?**

$480 ÷ 10 = 48$ and $48 ÷ 2 = 24$
so $480 ÷ 20$ is 24. £24 each.

? **What is the cost of a coach trip for one person?**

 **Coach Trip**
£960 for a party of 30

Task

The Avonford Star

Big lottery win for local syndicate

An Avonford syndicate has won the
lottery jackpot. They share £3 600 000.

? **What is a syndicate?**

Jo

How
much does each
person get?

How many
people were in
the syndicate?

Lucy

Make a table to show the share for different syndicate sizes.

Size	Share	Size	Share
60	£	30	£
50	£	25	£
40	£	24	£

? **How can you divide 45 000 by 150?**

Exercise

1 **(a)** Work out
   (i) 180 divided by 6
   (ii) the answer to part (i) divided by 3.
   (b) What is 180 ÷ 18?

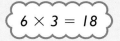

$6 \times 3 = 18$

2 **(a)** Work out
   (i) 420 divided by 5
   (ii) the answer to part (i) divided by 7.
   (b) What is 420 ÷ 35?

3 **(a)** Work out
   (i) 384 divided by 2
   (ii) the answer to part (i) divided by 4
   (iii) the answer to part (ii) divided by 3.
   (b) What is 384 ÷ 24?

4 Copy and complete the following crossword puzzle.

Across
1 217 ÷ 7
2 230 ÷ 5
3 540 ÷ 20
5 72 ÷ 24
6 90 ÷ 45
7 240 ÷ 30
8 15 100 ÷ 25

Down
1 72 ÷ 2
2 588 ÷ 14
4 2250 ÷ 30
6 1040 ÷ 40
7 5040 ÷ 60

Finishing off

Now that you have finished this chapter you should be able to:

- combine operations of addition, subtraction, multiplication, and division
- do long multiplication
- use factors to divide by larger numbers.

Review exercise

1 Work out these.

(a) $2 \times 3 + 5$ **(b)** $2 + 3 \times 5$ **(c)** $6 \times 2 - 1$
(d) $4 + 7 \times 5$ **(e)** $36 \div 4 - 2$ **(f)** $8 + 72 \div 8$

2 Which is bigger?

(a) $2 \times 3 + 7$ or $14 \div 2 + 5$ **(b)** $40 - 7 \times 4$ or $50 - 4 \times 9$
(c) $45 \div 9$ or $7 \times 3 - 15$

3 Work out these.

(a) $2 \times 3 + 7 \times 9$ **(b)** $20 \div 5 + 18 \div 6$
(c) $5 \times 8 - 3 \times 11$ **(d)** $72 \div 9 - 35 \div 7$

4 What is the cost of seats for

(a) one person

(b) two people?

Theatre Booking Agent
£700 *for 35 seats in block C*

5 Ali needs to give her cats some pills.

How many pills does she give Tabby and her kittens altogether?

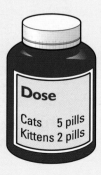

Dose
Cats   5 pills
Kittens 2 pills

6 Work out the average in each case.

(a) 3 magazines which cost £2.45, £1.80 and £3.25.

(b) Mark's test results in 5 subjects.

Geography 63	Maths 44	English 55
Science 33	CDT 65	

7 Work out these.

(a) (i) 6×7 (ii) 60×7 (b) (i) 6×70 (ii) 6×700
(c) (i) 9×8 (ii) 9×80 (d) (i) 90×8 (ii) 900×8

8 (a) Work out these.
   (i) 60×3
   (ii) 4×3
(b) What is 64×3?

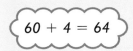
60 + 4 = 64

9 (a) Work out these.
   (i) 50×4
   (ii) 7×4
(b) What is 57×4?

10 Copy and complete these.

(a) $24 = 3 \times \;\;\;$ (b) $42 = 6 \times \;\;\;$

(c) $45 = 5 \times \;\;\;$ (d) $56 = 8 \times \;\;\;$

11 (a) Work out
   (i) $231 \div 3$
   (ii) the answer to part (i) divided by 7.
(b) What is $231 \div 21$?

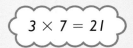
3 × 7 = 21

12 (a) Work out
   (i) $1323 \div 3$
   (ii) the answer to part (i) divided by 3.
   (iii) the answer to part (ii) divided by 7.
(b) What is $1323 \div 63$?

13 Do two or more divisions to work out these.

(a) $744 \div 24$ (b) $336 \div 42$

14 Work out $138\,432 \div 336$ using three or more divisions.

Answers

Here are the answers to the Review Exercises to help you to check your progress. All other answers are in the Teacher's Resource that goes with this book.

I   How our numbers work (pages 8–9)

I   **(a)** 60 294
(b) Six million, twenty nine thousand, four hundred

2   **(a)** Twenty million, nine hundred and seventy five thousand
(b) 2 097 500 → Two million, ninety seven thousand, five hundred

3   **(a)**

÷10	÷10 again	÷10 again
22 000	2200	220
1600	160	16
110 100	11 010	1101

(b)

×10	×10 again	×10 again
250	2500	25 000
8470	84 700	847 000
99 090	990 900	9 909 000

4   **(a)** 23 938   **(b)** 24 238   **(c)** 24 438   **(d)** 24 538
(e) 715 360   **(f)** 715 370   **(g)** 715 390   **(h)** 715 400

5   **(a)** Ask your teacher to check your answer.
(b) Ask your teacher to check your answer.
(c) Ask your teacher to check your answer.

6   **(a)** 9 886 431 → Nine million, eight hundred and eighty six thousand, four hundred and thirty one
(b) 1 346 889 → One million, three hundred and forty six thousand, eight hundred and eighty nine

7   **(a)** 3000 ml
(b) 20 litres lemonade, 4·5 litres (4500 ml) orange juice, 3 litres (3000 ml) grapefruit juice, $2\frac{1}{2}$ litres (2500 ml) pineapple juice.
(c) 12 glasses

2   Position (pages 14–15)

I   **(a)** **(i)** Meet me at the shops   **(ii)** Maths is cool
(iii) Come to my party   **(iv)** My dog is called Max
(b) Ask your teacher to check your answer.

2   C2

3   **(a)** 8   **(b)** D7   **(c)** F4 is the highlighted cell
(d) 63   **(e)** =SUM(E4:E8)

3   Basic number (pages 24–25)

I   **(a)** **(i)** 68   **(ii)** 97   **(iii)** 131   **(iv)** 60
(b) Kim has the highest score.

2   **(a)** 13p   **(b)** 9p   **(c)** 15p   **(d)** 37p

3   **(a)** 18   **(b)** 16   **(c)** 6   **(d)** 9

4   **(a)** 30 mm   **(b)** 580 mm   **(c)** 765 mm   **(d)** 185 mm

5   **(a)** 15   **(b)** 13   **(c)** 14   **(d)** 31

6

¹6		²3	9		³1
⁴1	⁵8	6		⁶2	8
	⁷1	4		8	
⁸4	0		⁹4	3	¹⁰1
¹¹4	9		¹²8	2	3
	0		¹³5	7	2

4   Angles (pages 32–33)

I   **(a)** B, C, E, D, A, F
(b) **(i)** A, D   **(ii)** F   **(iii)** B, C

2   A = 85°   B = 50°   C = 25°

3   Ask your teacher to check your angles.

4   **(a)** 2   **(b)** 4   **(c)** 3

5   **(a)** 90   **(b)** 360

6   3°, 53°, A right angle, An obtuse angle, A straight line, 240°, 300°.

7   Ask your teacher to check your angles.

8   Ask your teacher to check your rectangle.

5   Displaying data (pages 40–41)

I

Sandwich	Tally	Frequency
Beef	|||	3
Chicken	|||	3
Cheese	|||	3
Ham	ℍℍ ||	7
Prawn	|||	3
Salad	||	2
Total		21

2

Colour	Tally	Frequency
Red	ℍℍ ||||	9
Yellow	ℍℍ |||	8
Green	||||	4
Blue	||||	4
Total		25

3   **(a)** Ask your teacher to check your bar chart.
(b) 38

4   **(a)** June
(b) Ask your teacher to check your bar chart.

5   **(a)** Yes. It was sunny for two thirds of June.
(b) It was cloudy as often as it was wet or heavy rain. There was heavy rain less often than it was just wet.

6   Symmetry pages (pages 50–51)

I   **(a)**

						¹M	I	R	R	O	R
				²S	Q	U	A	R	E		
				³R	E	F	L	E	C	T	I	O	N
				⁴S	Y	M	M	E	T	R	Y		
							⁵A	X	I	S			
	⁶R	O	T	A	T	I	O	N					
						⁷D	I	A	G	O	N	A	L
							⁸L	I	N	E			
			⁹O	R	D	E	R						

(b) A rectangle has two lines of symmetry.

2   **(a)**

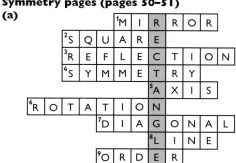

Note: if O is drawn as a circle, every diameter is a line of symmetry.

(b)

H order 2   I order 2   N order 2

⊙ order 2   S order 2   X order 2

Z order 2

Note: if O is drawn as a circle, it has complete rotational symmetry.

7 Decimals (pages 58–59)

I
4000	Four thousand
400	Four hundred
40	Forty
4	Four
0.4	Four tenths
0.04	Four hundredths

2 **(a)** 6.1 **(b)** 8.5 **(c)** 2.35
3 Ask your teacher to check your tables.

8 Co-ordinates (pages 64–65)

I **(a)** No **(b)** Yes
(c) (3, 3) Yes, (5, 3) Yes, (4, 2) Yes, (4, 4) No
(d) (0, 2), (1, 2), (2, 2) and (4, 0), (4, 1), (4, 2) and (1, 5), (2, 5), (3, 5) and (3, 3), (4, 3) and (5, 3)
2 A(2, 4), B(5, 4), C(4, 1), D(1, 1) and E(2, 5), F(4, 5), G(5, 3), H(4, 1), I(2, 1), J(1, 3)
3 **(a)** Ask your teacher to check your work. **(b)** (1, 5)
4 An elephant

9 Fractions (pages 74–75)

I **(a)** **(i)** 4 parts shaded **(ii)** 5 parts shaded
(b) 50%
(c) **(i)** $\frac{4}{8} = \frac{1}{2}$ **(ii)** $\frac{5}{10} = \frac{1}{2}$
2 **(a)** **(i)** 1 part shaded **(ii)** 2 parts shaded
(b) $\frac{2}{6}$
3 **(a)** **(i)** $\frac{1}{5}$ **(ii)** $\frac{3}{5}$ **(iii)** $\frac{4}{5}$
(b) $\frac{1}{5} = \frac{2}{10} = \frac{20}{100} = 20\%$
4 **(a)** 8 **(b)** 4 **(c)** 12
5 **(a)** **(i)** 50% **(ii)** 25% **(iii)** 75%
(b) **(i)** $\frac{1}{2}$ **(ii)** $\frac{1}{4}$ **(iii)** $\frac{3}{4}$
(c) **(i)** 50% **(ii)** 75% **(iii)** 25%
6 **(a)** 25 shaded **(b)** 10 shaded **(c)** 2 shaded
7 **(a)** 10 shaded **(b)** 5 shaded **(c)** 5 shaded

10 Types of number (pages 84–85)

I **(a)** 7, 9, 11, 15, 17, 21 **(b)** 4, 8, 12, 16, 24
(c) 4, 9, 16 **(d)** Any two of 4, 8 and 16
(e) 12 and 24 **(f)** 11 **(g)** 7 and 8
(h) 16, 9 and 7 **or** 15, 8 and 9 **or** 17, 11 and 4 **or** 17, 8 and 7 **or** 12, 16 and 4 **or** 12, 11 and 9
2 **(a)** 64 **(b)** 53 **(c)** 36
3 56
4

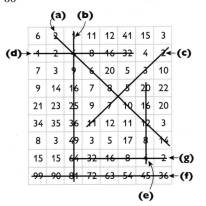

5

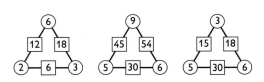

11 Everyday measures (pages 94–95)

I **(a)** Length: metre, centimetre, kilometre, millimetre
Weight: gram, kilogram
Capacity: millilitre, litre
(b) Length: mile, yard
Weight: ounce, stone
Capacity: gallon, pint
2 **(a)** Flour, butter, yeast, raisins and sugar.
(b) Milk and water.
3 **(a)** 100 g **(b)** 900 g
(c) 1300 g **or** 1.3 kg **(d)** 1700 g **or** 1.7 kg
4 **(a)** Centimetres **(b)** Kilometres
(c) Months, weeks or days **(d)** Centimetres
(e) Tonnes **(f)** Seconds
5 **(a)** **(i)** Twenty five minutes past six **(ii)** 6:25
(b) **(i)** Five minutes past eight **(ii)** 8:05
(c) **(i)** Twenty minutes to ten **(ii)** 9:40
(d) **(i)** Ten minutes to five **(ii)** 4:50
(e) **(i)** Twenty five minutes to seven **(ii)** 6:35
6 **(a)** 1930 **(b)** 1120 **(c)** 2055
(d) 1405 **(e)** 0535
7 **(a)** 35 minutes
(b) She gets on at Honiton and off at Feniton
(c) 55 minutes

12 Flat shapes (pages 102–103)

I **(a)** 1 cm, 1 cm, 1 cm   Equilateral
(b) 3 cm, 5.5 cm, 6.3 cm   Scalene
(c) 5.7 cm, 6.0 cm, 2.9 cm   Scalene
(d) 4 cm, 4 cm, 4 cm   Equilateral
(e) 5 cm, 3 cm, 5 cm   Isosceles
2 Ask your teacher to check your drawing.
3 **(a)** Ask your teacher to check your drawing.
(b) 3 cm
4 Ask your teacher to check your work.
5 Ask your teacher to check your work.

13 Multiplying and dividing decimals (pages 108–109)

I **(a)** 4.0 **(b)** 1.2 **(c)** 2.1 **(d)** 2.4
(e) 0.008 **(f)** 1.2 **(g)** 4.5 **(h)** 13.5
(i) 2.16 **(j)** 2.60 **(k)** 7.38 **(l)** 6.00
2 **(a)** 0.7 **(b)** 0.16 **(c)** 0.015 **(d)** 0.014
(e) 1.6 **(f)** 4.2 **(g)** 6.012 **(h)** 4.89
(i) 23.70 **(j)** 37.08 **(k)** 52.32 **(l)** 0.2415
3 **(a)** 50.4 **(b)** 64.8 **(c)** 54.60
(d) 57.36 **(e)** 6.836 **(f)** 0.138
4
Delivery vans	£16.20
Cars	£43.60
Trucks	£13.50
Letter boxes	£5.68
Mail vans	£22.00
Taxi cabs	£17.28
Total	£118.26

5
Jigsaws	£37.95
Books	£34.32
Games	£34.56
Total	£106.83

6 **(a)** 0.9 **(b)** 1.3 **(c)** 4.7
(d) 1.04 **(e)** 0.094 **(f)** 0.109

7 **(a)** 2.9 **(b)** 0.27 **(c)** 1.6
 (d) 0.13 **(e)** 0.82 **(f)** 1.2
8 **(a)** 96 **(b)** 12 years
9 **(a)** 108 **(b)** 12 years
10

4

14 Number machines (pages 118–119)

1

Number of miles	1	2	3	4	5	6	10
Fare (p)	100	130	160	190	220	250	370
Fare (£)	£1.00	£1.30	£1.60	£1.90	£2.20	£2.50	£3.70

2 **(a)** 15 **(b)** 35 **(c)** 8 **(d)** 15
 (e) 14 **(f)** 4 **(g)** 19 **(h)** 4
3 **(a)**

Number of hours → ×6 → +10 → Cost in pounds

 (b)

Time (hours)	1	2	3	4	6	8	10
Cost (£)	£16	£22	£28	£34	£46	£58	£70

4

Input	3	6	9	30	63
Output	1	2	3	10	21

5 **(a)** ×2 **(b) (i)** −2 **(ii)** ÷5

15 Scale drawing (pages 126–127)

1 **(a) (i)** 80 m **(ii)** 50 m **(iii)** 120 m **(iv)** 20 m
 (b) (i) 3 cm **(ii)** 2.5 cm **(iii)** 7 cm
2 **(a)** 250 cm (2.5 m) **(b)** 1.5 cm
3 **(a)** About 800 m **(b)** About 950 m
 (c) The shortest route is past the church. It is about 150 m shorter.

16 Averages (pages 134–135)

1 **(a)** 37 **(b)** 2
2 **(a)** 11 **(b)** 17
3 **(a)** 7 **(b)** 8.1
4 1.6
5 **(a)**

Car	Tally	Frequency
BMW			1
Ford	𝗡𝗡 ||	7
Peugeot	||	2
Renault	|||	3
Vauxhall	𝗡𝗡	5
Total		18

 (b) Ford
6 **(a)** 16 **(b)** 27
7 **(a) (i)** 22 minutes **(ii)** 21 minutes
 (b) (i) 20 minutes **(ii)** 21 minutes
 (c) Mr Jones
 (d) The mean

17 Formulae (pages 142–143)

1 **(a)** 90p **(b)** £1.20 **(c)** £3
2 **(a)** Price = 12 × number of CDs + 15 × number of DVDs
 (b) (i) £36 **(ii)** £30 **(iii)** £39 **(iv)** £93
3 **(a)** Cost (in pence) = 25 × number of minutes
 (b) John: 11 minutes Humza: 21 minutes

18 Negative numbers (pages 148–149)

1

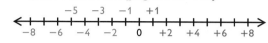

2 **(a)** +3 **(b)** −4 **(c)** +10 **(d)** −7
3

Temperature in morning (°C)	Change in temperature (°C)	Temperature in afternoon (°C)
+4	Up 2	+6
+3	Down 4	−1
−1	Up 5	+4
−2	Down 3	−5
−10	Up 8	−2
−3	Down 1	−4
0	Down 4	−4
+1	Up 4	+5
−2	Down 1	−3

4 **(a)** −1 **(b)** +2 **(c)** −5 **(d)** +1
 (e) −5 **(f)** −7 **(g)** 0 **(h)** −1
 (i) −6 **(j)** +1 **(k)** +9 **(l)** −8

19 Solid shapes (pages 154–155)

1 **(a) (i)** Cube **(ii)** Triangular prism
 (iii) Cuboid **(iv)** Hexagonal prism
 (v) Cuboid **(vi)** Cuboid
 (vii) Cuboid **(viii)** Triangular prism
 (ix) Octagonal prism **(x)** Cuboid
 (xi) Cuboid **(xii)** Cuboid
 (b) Cuboid
2 **(a)** Cuboid **(b)** Cuboid
 (c) On top of the first 4
3 **(b)** There are not two opposite end faces which are the same. There are no faces which are rectangles.
 (c) Tetrahedron: 4 faces, 6 edges, 4 vertices.
 Octahedron: 8 faces, 12 edges, 6 vertices.
 Both shapes obey Euler's Rule.
 (d) They are all equilateral triangles.

20 Graphs (pages 160–161)

1 **(a)** Ask your teacher to check your graph.
 (b) 18 °C
 (c) Saturday
 (d) 2°
 (e) Thursday
 (f) Always rises
2 **(a)** Ask your teacher to check your graph.
 (b) £46.70 (approx)
 (c) €37.50
 (d) £35.30 (approx)
3 **(a)** 68 °F **(b)** 32 °F
 (c) 24 °C **(d)** Between 7° and 8° Centigrade.
4 **(a)** 30 **(b)** 20 (not including weekends)
 (c) Saturday **(d)** 30

21 Measuring (pages 168–169)
1 (a) 36 m²   (b) 28 m
2 (a) 3 layers   (b) 8 cubes in one layer

22 Flow diagrams and number patterns (pages 180–181)
1 (a) 4, 8, 12, 16, 20, 24, 28, 32, 36, 40
  (b) Multiples of 4
  (c) 4
  (d) 44, 48
  (e) 80
  (f) 400
  (g) 70 is not a multiple of 4 **or** 70 is not in the 4 times table.
  (h) 72, 76, 80
2 (a)

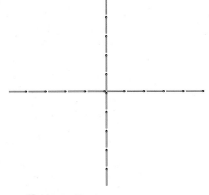

  (b)

Length of arm	1	2	3	4	5
Number of matchsticks	4	8	12	16	20

  (c) Increase by 4
  (d) One matchstick is added onto each of the 4 ends of the cross.
3 Not multiples of 4: 1, 2, 3, 5, 6, 7, 9, 10, 11, 13, 14, 15, 17, 18, 19
Multiples of 4: 4, 8, 12, 16, 20

23 Accuracy (pages 188–189)
1 (a) 40p   (b) 70p   (c) 10p   (d) £1.00
  (e) 60p   (f) £1.20   (g) £4.80
2

	Nearest 100	Nearest 10
371	400	370
402	400	400
6399	6400	6400
1045	1000	1050

3 (a) 10 mm   (b) 30 mm   (c) 40 mm
  (d) 80 mm   (e) 100 mm   (f) 110 mm
4 (a) 160 km   (b) 630 km   (c) 600 km
5 (a) £2.00   (b) £7.00   (c) £3.00   (d) £6.00
  (e) £4.00   (f) £8.00   (g) £10.00   (h) £15.00
  (i) £28.00   (j) £50.00

6 (a) £1.40   (b) £6.60   (c) £3.30
  (d) £12.40   (e) £8.70   (f) £26.10
7 (a) 109 km per hour   (b) 70 km per hour
  (c) 67 km per hour   (d) 2 km per hour
8 (a) 2 kg   (b) 3 kg   (c) 4 kg
  (d) 7 kg   (e) 7 kg   (f) 9 kg
9

Sum	Rough calculation	Rough answer	Accurate answer
31 + 49	30 + 50	80	80
29 + 44	30 + 40	70	73
65 − 49	70 − 50	20	16
23 + 37	20 + 40	60	60
62 − 48	60 − 50	10	14

10 (a) 2   (b) 8   (c) 16
  (d) 3   (e) 30   (f) 3

24 Probability (pages 194–195)
1 (a) Likely **or** impossible (for example, if it is a Friday)
  (b) Unlikely
  (c) Evens
  (d) Certain
  (e) Unlikely
  (f) Likely
2 (a) $\frac{1}{7}$ (b) $\frac{4}{7}$ (c) $\frac{3}{7}$
  (d) 1   (e) 0   (f) $\frac{2}{7}$
3 (a) 10   (b) $\frac{1}{10}$
4 (a) $\frac{1}{6}$ (b) $\frac{5}{12}$ (c) $\frac{5}{12}$

25 Operations (pages 202–203)
1 (a) 11   (b) 17   (c) 11
  (d) 39   (e) 7   (f) 17
2 (a) $2 \times 3 + 7$ is bigger (13 is bigger than 12)
  (b) $50 - 4 \times 9$ is bigger (14 is bigger than 12)
  (c) $7 \times 3 - 15$ is bigger (6 is bigger than 5)
3 (a) $6 + 63 = 69$ (b) $4 + 3 = 7$
  (c) $40 - 33 = 7$ (d) $8 - 5 = 3$
4 (a) £20   (b) £40
5 17
6 (a) £2.50   (b) 52
7 (a) (i) 42   (ii) 420
  (b) (i) 420   (ii) 4200
  (c) (i) 72   (ii) 720
  (d) (i) 720   (ii) 7200
8 (a) (i) 180   (ii) 12   (b) 192
9 (a) (i) 200   (ii) 28   (b) 228
10 (a) 8   (b) 7
  (c) 9   (d) 7
11 (a) (i) 77   (ii) 11
  (b) 11
12 (a) (i) 441   (ii) 147   (iii) 21
  (b) 21
13 (a) 31   (b) 8
14 412